Why Asia?

Contemporary Asian and Asian American Art

Why Asia?
Contemporary Asian and Asian American Art

Alice Yang

Edited by Jonathan Hay and Mimi Young

NEW YORK UNIVERSITY PRESS
New York and London

New York University Press
New York and London

Design by Lisa Billard Design, New York

Library of Congress Cataloging-in-Publication Data
Yang, Alice, 1961-1997.
    Why Asia? : contemporary Asian and Asian American art /
    Alice Yang ; edited by Jonathan Hay and Mimi Young.
        p. cm.
    Includes bibliographical references.
    ISBN 0-8147-3579-7
    1. Art, Asian. 2. Art, Modern—20th century—Asia. 3. Asian
American art. 4. Art, Modern—20th century—United States.
I. Hay, Jonathan Scott. II. Young, Mimi, 1967- . III. Title.
N7260.Y36 1997
709'.5'0904—dc21   97-33892
                              CIP

Contents

Foreword

The current upsurge in interest in Asian artists throughout the contemporary art field is hard to miss. Their work is found with increasing frquency in museums, mainstream galleries, and alternative spaces. And although the degree to which Asian American artists are sharing in this new attention is uncertain, the changed climate engages and affects these artists as well. It is increasingly clear that contemporary Asian and Asian American art alike pose particular challenges to artists, critics, curators and viewers, and stand in need of more informed criticism. Beginning in 1993, Alice Yang accumulated a sustained body of critical work, unique in its attention to both sides of the "Asian" equation. With the author's characteristic sensitivity to cultural differences, Yang provides a more complex understanding of the multiple contexts in which we view and think about contemporary Asian and Asian American art. *Why Asia?* brings together the full range of her writings in this area, making available an essential contribution to contemporary criticism.

It should be noted that a small number of essays include fragments of similar text. These essays were originally written within divergent contexts: as a conference paper, an exhibition brochure, an article for an Asian periodical. In the absence of the author, the editors have chosen to preserve the writer's voice and present these essays unaltered.

We owe our deepest gratitude to the parents, husband, and brothers of Alice Yang—Mrs. Suhwa Chou Yang and Mr. William H.Y. Yang, Gerald Szeto, and Andrew and James Yang—without whose commitment and support this publication would not have been possible.

We offer our sincere thanks to Russell Ferguson for providing invaluable insight and advice throughout the project; to Eric Zinner of New York University Press for welcoming the project to the Press; to Lisa Billard of Lisa Billard Design, NY, for an elegant and timely publication design; to Christine Giviskos for her administrative assistance; and to the many colleagues of Alice Yang who encouraged us to pursue this project, especially Lynn Gumpert and Robert Lubar. Special appreciation goes to Susan Acret at ART AsiaPacific; Francesca Dal Lago; Elizabeth Finch of The Drawing Center; Marcia Tucker and the staff of The New Museum of Contemporary Art; and Lydia Yee of The Bronx Museum of the Arts, for their cooperation and research assistance with many aspects of this publication. Finally, we would like to acknowledge the artists, galleries, museums and publications that generously provided visual materials and granted permission to reprint many of the essays in this volume.

Jonathan Hay and Mimi Young, New York 1997

Four Artists

Letting Go: The Work of Rirkrit Tiravanija

For those who wandered into 303 Gallery in New York this June,[1] there was nothing to see. No paintings, no drawings, not anything that could qualify as a conventional art object. Instead, led by an enticing aroma emanating from the back room, visitors discovered a makeshift kitchen and a meal free for the taking. With bags of groceries scattered about, dining tables set up, and two pots of Thai curry simmering on burners, 303 Gallery became the setting for the most basic and pleasurable of activities—eating—and the convivial socializing that comes with it.

1
Originally on view May 20 –
July 8, 1995. Eds.

303 had not abandoned its gallery operations. The meal was offered courtesy of the Thai artist Rirkrit Tiravanija, who took turns with a friend to cook every day at the gallery for his six-week-long project. Food has become a signature component of Tiravanija's work since the late 1980s, but he is a cook not so much of meals but of situations. A pot of curry for eating, a bar for drinking, a couch for sitting, a tent for resting—from these humble ingredients, Tiravanija creates a space in the gallery or museum in which people can slow down, find some nourishment and interact with others. In so doing, the artist has sought to make room for (or at least remind us of) those experiences which are usually deemed foreign to the art context. Like his previous works, *Untitled, 1995 (Still)* at 303 tested the boundary between art and everyday life, between the consumption of art and the fulfillment of elementary needs.

Rirkrit Tiravanija
Untitled, 1995 (Still)
Installation view, 303 Gallery, New York
Courtesy 303 Gallery, New York

Tiravanija has become a frequent participant in major international exhibitions in the last few years, including the 1993 Venice Biennale and the 1995 Carnegie International. That so many curators and critics have embraced his work says something about present-day doldrums. As one critic describes it, Tiravanija's work is "user-friendly."[2] It has an artlessness that is a refreshing change from the relentlessly artful. His work responds to those simple longings and offers those authentic connections that seem increasingly elusive in a time of international art spectacles, e-mail, and peripatetic travel.

But Tiravanija's work is grounded in much more than these immediate gratifications. Its strategy is one of unexpected dislocations. At the Rooseum in Sweden in 1995, for example, Tiravanija created a scaled-down house in which children from the museum's daycare center would be allowed to come and play. Likewise, at the Walker Art Center in Minneapolis later the same year, Tiravanija set up a tent with a couch and provided a "meditation area" with blankets, enabling museum visitors to sit down and rest. The room featured, among other things, an audio tape of a weekly Hmong radio program and a video about the production of Hmong appliqué pieces, which made reference to the large community of Hmongs who have been displaced from their native Laos and resettled in the Minneapolis area.

Rirkrit Tiravanija
Untitled, 1995 (Back of postcard reads:)
Mixed media installation
Collection Walker Art Center, Minneapolis
Gift of the artist, 1995

Each of these projects, taking the shape of a temporary structure, transposed a different physical and social space into the institutional site of art.

[2]
Holland Cotter, "A Critic's Dozen to Catch at the Biennial," *The New York Times*, 12 March 1995.

4

Rirkrit Tiravanija
Untitled, 1995 (Back of postcard reads:)
(detail of "meditation area")

Tiravanija's work creates a spatial dissonance which prompts our reflection about the established parameters of the art arena and the ways in which we conventionally "inhabit" it (look but don't touch). At the same time, it also allows us to recognize and re-evaluate the space of daily life and what is often taken for granted in it—work, sustenance, repose, play, conversation. While it seems to collapse the experience of art with the fundamental experience of life, Tiravanija's work is also a measure of their customary separation. It brings into relief the threshold that divides these two realms, where one begins and the other ends.

It is fitting, then, that windows have figured significantly in Tiravanija's work. In *Untitled, 1995 (Still)* at 303, for example, Tiravanija not only transformed the gallery into a communal kitchen, he also wrought subtle changes in its architecture. He unhinged doors from storage closets and uncovered windows that had been boarded up. Through this sleight-of-hand, Tiravanija invited us to look more deeply at what is inside the gallery as well as what lies outside of it.

Tiravanija's work is delicately poised at such a threshold, with a view towards what is on either side of it. As he suggested in a recent article co-authored with the English artist Liam Gillick, his work may be thought of as a parallel to what happens in life, not a simple substitute for it. "Parallel positions may be the real center of activity," they write. "It is possible that there is more space for things to happen within this

3
Rirkrit Tiravanija and Liam
Gillick, "Forget about the Ball
and Get on with the Game,"
Parkett, no. 44 (1995), p. 108.

exchange, because it is never 'really real' but another fiction. It is not possible to be really real within the parameters we are involved in."[3] Nonetheless, as they explain, their approach allows for a shift in focus and a different type of engagement: "Something quite normal. Not authentic, just normal . . . Places where there is still some room to maneuver."

photo: Dan Cameron

Rirkrit Tiravanija
Untitled (from Barajas to Paracuellos del Jarama, to Torrejón de Ardoz to Coslada and to Reina Sofía), 1994
Mixed media
Courtesy Dan Cameron

The passage between outside and inside took yet another form in two of Tiravanija's recent projects. At the 1994 group exhibition *Cocido y Crudo* in Madrid, Tiravanija showed a mini-video which documented his bicycle trip from the airport to the exhibition site, along with a catalogue of all the meals and meetings that took place in-between. For the Kwangju Biennale in Korea in 1995, Tiravanija embarked on a longer pilgrimage, traveling non-stop, by foot and by train, for five days around Korea visiting old temples. Recording the journey with a camera attached to his backpack, Tiravanija produced a forty-hour-long video-tape which was shown in its entirety during the exhibition.

In both of these projects, video becomes the metaphorical window onto the outside world, providing a glimpse of the multiplicity of its textures and rhythms. Tiravanija offers us a reminder of how it is experienced, how its quotidian details accrue and unfold in time. These projects evoke the breadth and duration of an experience that cannot be fully contained within the walls of the museum. It can only be transferred piecemeal via recorded images on videotape.

Nevertheless, Tiravanija's projects for Madrid and Kwangju share much in common with his other works. What is central to Tiravanija's art practice is a type of engagement or involvement that extends beyond the video to be viewed or the food to be consumed. Typically, this takes the form of a participatory situation which is activated by members of the audience. Tiravanija's contribution to the Johannesburg Biennial in 1995 was just such a situation conjured from the simplest of means. Along with two other artists, he orchestrated an afternoon soccer match in the parking lot of the exhibition grounds, which brought together the local team and participants in the Biennial. As he explained, he hoped to achieve through the game what he thought was the primary purpose of bringing artists from all over the world to Johannesburg. A soccer game, a meal, a concert, or a rest area thus become the framework for a communal experience and a social exchange. Tiravanija explains this idea with a succinct motto: "Forget the ball and get on with the game."[4]

4
Ibid.

A similar spirit of engagement informs his projects for Madrid and Kwangju. Tracing step by step Tiravanija's own interactions with a new surrounding, they reflect not only one person's journey but also an alternative model of the art-making process. Here, the production of some seductive art object is no longer at issue; rather, it is the making of dialogues and discoveries along the way which is key. Ultimately, Tiravanija's work is concerned with a mode of making—a way of generating meaning and of fostering understanding—with the most expansive potentials. Grounded in a philosophical attitude that is open to all and extends to all spheres, Tiravanija's record of his own journey becomes an allegory for life's journeys.

For Tiravanija, the project which he produced for the Kwangju Biennale was also a response to the theme of internationalism and globalization chosen for the exhibition. He is wary of notions of a global culture because, as he explains, "as much as everything is much more open, it is also closed."[5] Tiravanija thus chose to produce a work that would situate him more intimately within a local rather than global context. "I decided to just go and walk through the country," he explains. "For me it was a solution to just bringing a foreign object and putting it in a room and letting people deal with that. I had to deal with the place."

5
Interview with the author, November 8, 1995, New York City. Unless otherwise noted, all other quotes by the artist are from this interview.

Cultural and geographical distance is something with which Tiravanija has had to contend for much of his life. Born in Argentina in 1961, he moved at the age of three to Thailand, where he lived intermittently between short stays in Ethiopia and Malaysia. Finishing high school in Thailand, he left to pursue an art education in Canada and settled in the mid-1980s in New York where he now lives.

The Thai curry which is often featured as part of Tiravanija's work speaks of his embrace of Thai culture as an integral aspect of his biography. Tiravanija's nomadic existence has, nonetheless, deeply influenced his views about the fluidity of such identities. As he notes, since he works largely in the U.S. and in Europe, he often lacks the right ingredients to make an authentic curry for his projects. Far from resistant to these constraints, Tiravanija sees his concoctions as an apt metaphor for the process of hybridization in culture as well as the experience of removal and loss that shapes the relationship to one's cultural roots.

Tiravanija explored these issues in more overt fashion at the 1993 Venice Biennale. His installation, composed of two cookers in an aluminum boat and a stockpile of Cup-O-Noodles, alluded to Marco Polo's voyage to the Orient and the often repeated mythology that he "discovered" noodles in China. The Cup-O-Noodles, "Oriental Style Instant Noodles" marketed to Western consumers, were made available for exhibition visitors to eat, thus setting the process of cultural consumption and cross-pollination into further motion.

These concerns notwithstanding, Tiravanija remains deeply committed to his homeland. He was thus disappointed when he was identified in a recent exhibition catalogue as an artist not from Thailand but the U.S. "My position all along has been that I would go back," he declares. "I'm just accumulating all my ideas before I go back, because I feel there's a lot to do there." Given the nature of Tiravanija's practice, it is not surprising that he sees his future goals in Thailand in terms that go beyond the purely artistic. Defining his role as both "artist and citizen," Tiravanija sees expanded possibilities for what he might accomplish. "[Thailand] is different politically, socially, culturally," he notes. "Within all those things, I think there's a lot of room to move around and make a difference."

For Tiravanija, Thai culture and society are matters of such internal attachments and resolutions. Although manifest in some of his works, Tiravanija has opted in many other instances not to make his cultural identity a visible marker. While wedded to the concept of homeland,

Tiravanija is concerned more broadly with the crossing of borders—with how each of us is embedded within particular cultural and social frameworks and how we might re-situate ourselves in relation to them in more open, mobile and liberatory ways.

It is on such a structural level that Tiravanija discerns his closest link to Thai culture. Increasingly, he has come to recognize the impact of Buddhism on his thinking and practice. He has alluded to this spiritual orientation in some of his projects by painting the walls of a room or using a tent in the same orange color as the robes worn by monks in Thailand. As Tiravanija notes, Buddhism is about "letting go." It is about an emancipation of the most radical kind: "Letting go of physicality and this object world."

Tiravanija's work withholds itself from our material grasp. Ephemeral and ever-changing, it draws us instead into a space and time that are constituted by our enactment of essential everyday activities, by our encounters with others, and by our reflection on these experiences. In this, it runs counter to the dominant logic governing art and modern-day capitalism. As one anthropologist has proposed, there is a deep affinity between trade and art from the point of view of material life: "Both involve what might be called the intensification of objecthood."[6] Tiravanija's work, in contrast, de-intensifies and dissolves our attachment to such objects.

6
Arjun Appadurai, *The Social Life of Things: Commodities in Cultural Perspective* (Cambridge: Cambridge University Press, 1986), p. 59.

In Buddhism, the object world is a world of insatiable cravings which frustrate and imprison us. Tiravanija's work, too, asks us to think about the tyranny of unquenchable desires so that we may focus on the importance of shared necessities. Although food is consumed at Tiravanija's projects, it is a basic nourishment that leaves only a temporary trace. "We are always measuring ourselves by what we have,"

Tiravanija says. "And we have to think about it, especially within the context of making art. The question is: Is it necessary or is it not?" This attention to the question of necessity is one reason why Tiravanija undertook *Untitled, 1995 (Still)* at 303 Gallery. The project was, with some differences, largely a reprise of a work called *Untitled, 1992 (Free)*

Rirkrit Tiravanija
Untitled, 1992 (Free)
Installation view, 303 Gallery, New York
Courtesy 303 Gallery, New York

at the same gallery three years earlier. When asked why he repeated himself, Tiravanija noted the expectation within a gallery system that an artist show up with some new idea every two years: "At the same time, I had the idea of, well, what is necessary? As much as it's set up exactly the same, it's never the same. Different people are in it."

More than just a daily staple, food is also an agent of social bonding in Tiravanija's work. Offered freely, it is circulated so that we too become part of a communal exchange. If the consumption of art commodities is about an economics of limited supply-and-demand, Tiravanija's work is about a metaphysics of constant give-and-take. Generous and inclusive in spirit, Tiravanija's work opens the way for the possibilities of a different regime of value.

1996

MSG: The Processed Art of Michael Joo

Michael Joo
Video still from *Remasculation Triptych* videos

Monosodium Glutamate, the food additive otherwise known as MSG, found its way from the kitchen into the gallery with the work of Michael Joo. Indeed, the artist may be credited with putting this substance to use—in ways and in quantities—barely imagined before. Huge industrial-sized bags of it are stacked casually one on top of another, their granular contents spilling out from torn openings, the sacks taking on a kind of slack sculptural presence. MSG has also assumed a performative dimension in Joo's work. In 1994 the artist made a video of himself swimming in two-thousand-pounds-worth of the stuff.

MSG is only one of the many ingredients of Joo's art, but it provides a revealing introductory taste of his conceptual and iconographic repertoire. A product of laboratory experimentation—its frosty, crystalline appearance is reminiscent of other more sinister chemicals—MSG is allied in Joo's work with a broad exploration of the role of science and technology in contemporary life. A substance known to induce a range of vexing physical reactions, from headaches to sweating and chills, MSG points to Joo's preoccupation with the body, its processes, effects, and breakdowns. MSG, of course, is most often associated with Asian food, at least in the popular American imagination in which the term "Chinese restaurant syndrome" is in currency. In this, MSG suggests a racially tinged discourse of stereotyping and mistrust which is also a target in the work of this Korean American artist. Michael Joo's art, sometimes densely layered to the point of teasing complexity, lies somewhere at the intersection of all of these concerns.

That MSG has a tarnished reputation—as something disagreeable, unhealthy, and just plain inauthentic—is also played upon in Joo's work. Used in processed foods, MSG is dubbed a "flavor enhancer" by some advertisers. ("Put the accent on!" is the slogan of one U.S. brand.) Joo, in turn, calls MSG a "meaning enhancer" in his work.[1] Although he intends the term quite literally, it is telling that Joo speaks not of "meaning" but of a "meaning enhancer," as if "meaning" itself needed a bit of a boost. The intervening gap is indicative of Joo's somewhat skeptical attitude towards stable truths. Joo is instead interested in the constant slippages and transfers in meaning generated through an ongoing cycle of circulation, consumption, and exchange. In Joo's work, meaning—and matter—lose their distinct, abiding contours. Set into process, they ricochet wildly like the balls in a pinball machine.

1
Joo used this term specifically in relation to the work *Miss Megook* of 1993 in an interview with the author on February 21, 1996. All subsequent quotes by Joo are from this interview, unless otherwise noted.

MSG made its appearance in Joo's first solo exhibition in New York, at the Nordanstad-Skarsdet Gallery in 1992, alongside an assortment of other physical residues including urine, salt blocks, and synthetic tears.[2] These elemental substances were paired in the installation with sleek industrial materials such as aluminum, giving the exhibition the decided feel of a construction site-cum-laboratory. Central to the exhibition was the paradigm of science itself and the language of authority that science so often assumes.

In *Slanty—The Angle of Identification (73,864 cal.)*, for example, a prominent piece in the 1992 exhibition, Joo created a minimalist sculpture in the form of a three-dimensional pie chart. Each wedge in the chart purports to measure the angle of the eye, from the lower to the upper part of the lid, of various personalities in the popular media including Imelda Marcos, Yul Brynner, and Frank Oz (the puppeteer of the yellow-colored puppet Bert from *Sesame Street*). These measurements are in turn gauged in relation to the angle of the artist's own eyes (29.38) inscribed on top of each wedge, which also contains small amounts of synthetic tears. In *Slanty*, Joo appropriates the techniques of science to reveal its own "slant" behind a facade of impartiality, exposing the fine line between so-called factual knowledge and stereotypical myths. More broadly, as the artist notes himself, he is concerned with the question, "Who has the authority to say what?"

Joo's sensibility is, however, quite dead-pan. Perhaps this is because the artist seems to approach science with a kind of exactitude and seriousness that belies his unorthodox aims. This tactic is exemplified in *Operational Myth #3*, a work which employs caloric equations as a conceptual motif and the laws of physics as a sculptural paradigm—two devices that have become constants in Joo's oeuvre. One in a series of three related pieces, it is composed, at one end, of an aluminum expan-

2
The gallery was reorganized and renamed as the Thomas Nordanstad Gallery.

15

sion rod, which is used to hold a chalkboard in place against the ceiling, and at the other of a stack of salt blocks placed on an aluminum tray on the floor. Etched on the tray is a description of the cosmetic surgery called "Double Eye Plasty," undergone primarily by Asian women who want to "Occidentalize" their eyes. Next to this is inscribed the number of calories supposedly consumed by the artist in the making of the piece. (24,503 calories in total for the three "Myths," according to Joo's own precise if idiosyncratic calculations.)

Energy—its expenditure, flow, and combustion—becomes in the *Operational Myth* series, as in Joo's other works, both a tangible gauge and an abstract metaphor for the volatile nature of social exchange. Just as the pressure of the aluminum rod physicalizes the contact points and stress lines of cross-cultural interactions in a sculpture so precariously propped up, so the caloric calculations literalize Joo's own consumption and reproduction of racial myths as an Asian American man. Like a zealous scientist, Joo re-tabulates and re-engineers highly fraught issues of racial identification, so that they can be reckoned afresh. As a result the charged content of his work jostles against its seemingly impassive mode of presentation, creating a curious friction. As Joo observed in a 1993 interview: "With the Nordanstad show, I felt it was really crucial to distill everything down, particularly in the arena of identity, into a non-dramatic moment, something free of so much subjective viewpoint."[3] The expenditure of energy thus becomes a displaced measure of cultural values and conflicts. While imparting an aura of seeming objectivity, the distillation of complex issues of identification into numerical calculations and abstract formal structures renders them all the more elusive and untenable. Likewise, the body, the primary site of one's identity, evaporates into near nothingness here. What remains are only salt blocks, synthetic tears, and other ephemeral physical residues.

3
Roddy Bogawa and Michael Joo, "Exchange/Expansion/ Expenditure," *Documents* (New York) 1, no. 3 (summer 1993), p. 37.

In Joo's second solo project in New York in 1994, *Salt Transfer Cycle*, the artist expended energy in more visible and dynamic ways. As its centerpiece, the installation featured an arresting video that depicted Joo's

photo: Larry Lamay

Michael Joo
Salt Transfer Cycle, 1993-1994
Installation and *Remasculation Triptych* videos
Courtesy Petzel-Borgmann and Thomas Nordanstad Gallery, New York

enactment of a series of unusual and daunting physical feats. Divided into three sequences, the video begins with Joo swimming in two thousand pounds of MSG. It cuts next to images of him crawling, walking, then sprinting across the arid expanse of the salt flats in Utah, in a metaphorical evolution from amphibian, to primate, to *Homo sapiens*. The video ends with Joo sitting placidly on a mountain in Korea, surrounded by elks licking salt off his naked body.

These animated sequences were set off against a display of static objects in the installation which wove resonant associations with Joo's performance on screen. A sleek speed car, hand-carved from foam, harked back to the history of the Utah salt flats as the place where speed records have been set. (The car is modeled on one called The Blue Flame, which briefly held the world record in 1970. A video of this run was also shown on an accompanying monitor.) A row of elk antlers, cast in rubber, lined the walls on top of trays inscribed with the words "potency," "longevity," "vigor," and "desire" in reference to the practice in Korea and other Asian countries of ingesting powdered elk antlers as a drug to heighten these states.

A work of multilayered allusions, *Salt Transfer Cycle* draws seemingly disparate elements together to address intricate issues of male sexuality, evolutionary progress, and biological identity. It is, on one level, a self-mocking exercise in the hyper-performance of sexual and gender attributes—traits particularly called into doubt by popular stereotypes of Asian males. Like the run of The Blue Flame, a car noticeably phallic in shape, Joo's physical exertions have a he-man quality of daring heroics. Such presumptions of male prowess are, however, deflated in the exhibition by the flaccidity of the antlers and the car, reconstituted in synthetic materials like foam and rubber. As the artist points out, speed cars like The Blue Flame are "point-oriented but not really goal-oriented. Bam. It's just one huge expenditure of energy for nothing."

At the same time, *Salt Transfer Cycle* interrogates and pushes at the limits of the corporeal self. In the video the artist's body mutates through various states, not only along an evolutionary model but, even more fundamentally, on a molecular level. The body itself becomes a test site, a porous membrane through which MSG, sweat, salt, and saliva are exchanged in a constant cycle of transference. Disintegrating the very basis of an authentic, integrated self, Joo underscores the fluidity of cultural as well as physical identities.

That Joo's work is filled with references to the likes of Yul Brynner, The Blue Flame, and the *Sesame Street* puppet Bert reflects the artist's penchant for the icons of American popular culture. This sensibility may be viewed, perhaps, as a distinctive product of his background. Born in 1966 in the town of Ithaca, New York, Joo is a second-generation Korean American. As the artist describes it, his upbringing involved a jumbled mix of the high and the low, the Asian and the Western.

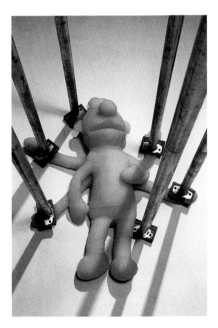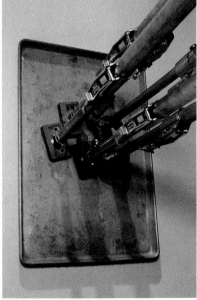

Michael Joo
Shiv-Shiva (762 cal. at 66 p.s.i.), 1993 (details)
    Aluminum pressure bars, cast rubber, ben-wa ball, synthetic testicle,
    lychee nut, synthetic sweat
    48 x 300 x 36"
    Courtesy The New Museum of Contemporary Art, New York

Questions of racial identity constitute only one facet of Joo's work. Like a Rubik's cube, it is composed of multiple, shifting parts which do not comply with a simple geometry. Self and body, abstract knowledge and material experience, biological transformation and technological change—all of these issues and many more form the elaborate matrix of Joo's art. The technological, in particular, was highlighted in Joo's 1995 exhibition at London's Anthony d'Offay Gallery. Entitled *Crash (A Failed Ascetic)*, the exhibition consisted of three sculptures that addressed the failures of science, industry, and religion respectively.

The first piece, *CRASH (Computer discs)*, comprises two computer discs, held apart by a suspension rod to form the shape of two splitting cells. Encased in resin, the disks are scratched to cause their so-called crash. *Rice Burner (Split Sled Triumph Rickshaw)* takes the form of cast rubber motorcycle engines modeled after those manufactured by the British company Triumph. The exhaust pipes, molded in Plexiglas and extended into expansion rods, are filled with MSG, a bag of which is also split open between the engines, as if ripped by the impact of their collision. *Ascetic/Acetic (Broken Arm Shiva)* is made up of

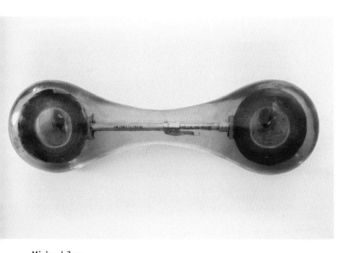

Michael Joo
CRASH (Computer discs), 1995
Cast polyester resin, engraved expansion rod, computer discs
66 x 12 x 18"
Courtesy Anthony d'Offay Gallery, London

seven aluminum limbs cast from Joo's own body to form the outlines of a dismembered Shiva, the Hindu god, along with glass vials of rice wine and thin aluminum rods inserted into each limb.

Joo's glossary of references for each of these works, as alluded to in their polysyllabic titles, is intricate and wide-ranging, as always. It encompasses everything from motorcycle lore to the chemical properties of wine. For *Rice Burner*, for example, Joo had in mind the history of Triumph motorcycles, once considered the finest until they were made obsolete by cheaper, more efficient Japanese bikes. The clogging of the engines' exhaust pipes with MSG thus represents the disruption of British industrial ascendancy by its Asian competitors. While such facts are illuminating, the significance of *Crash* may be grasped perhaps on a more basic level as well. That Joo named his exhibition after J.G. Ballard's celebrated 1973 novel, *Crash*, is telling. The novel revolves around a series of car accidents, which are represented as occasions for intoxicating experiences of power, speed, and sexuality. Joo's exhibition, offering up a terrain of broken bodies and dysfunctional machines, seems to share in a similarly dark vision.

Still, Joo's work is not entirely dystopic. Things may crash but, once bent out of shape, they also take on unexpected, potentially more versatile forms. Gas is exchanged for MSG, and blood is exchanged for wine. Machines become rubbery and organic, and bodies become hard and metallic. As in many of Joo's other works, *Crash* is distinguished by the mutability and interchangeability of its material forms—fluids and crystals, organic matters and synthetic residues. And here, it is perhaps more apt to quote, not J.G. Ballard, but the French theorist Paul Virilio, who writes about the contemporary culture of speed.

The new primacy of an accident—conceived in all of its instanta-
neous, energetic power—is no longer thought of as some sort of
deformation, some kind of destructive danger. Instead it becomes
a formation, a productive and constructive probability. . . . It is a
transference accident that challenges all primary references—such
as the unity of place and time—in favor of the motion of motion.[4]

4
Paul Virilio, *Lost Dimension*
(New York: Semiotext(e),
1991), p. 96.

Like *Crash*, Joo's most recent solo exhibition, which opened in April 1996
at New York's Thomas Nordanstand Gallery, evokes the collision of bodies
and objects in "the motion of motion." In *Landscape (subservience of
physical aggression to an emotionally laden conceptual framework)*, a
video still of the artist—shot from above and magnified to gargantuan

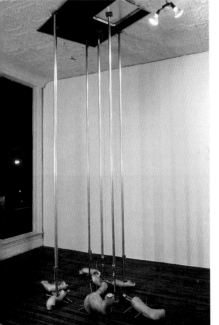

scale—is stretched across a trampoline frame
attached to the wall, creating an unsettling effect
of both dynamism and arrest, as if the body is at
once catapulting off the trampoline and trapped by
it. (The still is derived from a live video incorporated in another exhibition piece, which shows Joo
actually jumping on a trampoline.) Here, too, Joo
has reworked his *Broken Arm Shiva*, reconstructing it
with expansion rods which extend from the ceiling
to press against the metallic prosthetic limbs. If
motion is released only to be held in check in a
piece like *Landscape*, the exertion of pressure
appears to both shatter and buttress the bodily
fragments of the *Broken Arm Shiva*. In both literal

Michael Joo
Broken Arm Shiva, 1996
Cast aluminum, synthetic slate, aluminum
expansion rods, glass, aluminum tray, rice wine
168 x 96 x 72"

photo: Larry Lamay

and metaphorical ways, then, Joo traces tautly the arc of energy that is strained just at the breaking point and poised, to quote Virilio, at the edge between its "destructive danger" and its "constructive probability."

The animate states of energy and motion link up with concepts of transformation, which Joo discusses often in speaking about his work. "I'm interested in transformation for what comes in between two states. I'm interested in figuring out the moment of reaction, or the moment between growing up being called a 'Nip' and then seeing 'Cheese Nips.' I am interested in that moment in-between," he says, with his characteristic flair for unusual figures of speech. Transformation, then, is that space which opens up as conventional categories and perceptions begin to collide and dissolve, now more than ever with the swift changes wrought by science and technology. "With all of this manipulation of time and space now, cause-and-effect relations and one-two relations don't mean as much anymore," he says. "I don't see it as repressive. I'm just saying that two doesn't have to follow one anymore."

Joo's work, to borrow Virilio's words again, explores "the loss of sensible referents and the dissolution of various 'standards'" in the culture of our time.[5] This is where Joo's interest in the measures of science, the categories of race, and the expenditure of energy may be seen to converge. For energy becomes a fuel for and a trace of the possible transformation of previously fixed standards. In this way, Joo has fashioned a new type of process art for the 1990s—an art concerned with how identity, experience, knowledge, and the physical world have been processed before and how they may be reprocessed anew.

5
Virilio (1991), p. 140.

1996

Xu Bing: Rewriting Culture

*In the continual trauma that is "modernity," the question that
returns to haunt the Chinese intellectual is that of the continuity and
(re)production of Chinese culture. . . . How is culture—in ruins—to
be passed on, by whom, and with what means.* [1]

1
Rey Chow, "Pedagogy, Trust,
Chinese Intellectuals in the
1990s: Fragments of a Post-
Catastrophic Discourse," in
*Writing Diaspora: Tactics of
Intervention in Contemporary
Cultural Studies* (Bloomington
and Indianapolis: Indiana
University Press, 1993), p. 74.

The twentieth century has been a period of turbulent, cataclysmic change
in China. The effort to transform the country from a crippled empire into
a modern nation has involved painful and often disruptive political and
social adjustments. In their wake, Chinese culture has been left, to adopt
the words of the critic Rey Chow, "in ruins." This is a culture whose consciousness has been besieged on many fronts. Although a source of pride,
it has also been deemed inadequate to the demands of a modern society,
opened to dispute and censure by ever-fluctuating political agendas, as
well as profoundly challenged by the dominance of the West.

The work of Xu Bing may be understood against this backdrop. Born in
China in 1955 and a U.S. resident since 1990, Xu Bing has, for much of
his career, addressed the tangled legacy of his cultural heritage. His
work takes as its central organizing principle the structures of verbal
language, beginning with that of the Chinese language. While doing so,
however, Xu Bing has consistently subverted and undermined their com-
municative function. Xu Bing's is an art that simultaneously mourns and
embraces the loss of meaning and the instabilities of knowledge. In this
way, he returns again and again to the topos of a culture on the brink
between ruin and regeneration.

The seeds for these concerns first appeared in *A Book from the Sky*, a
monumental installation which Xu Bing initially produced in Beijing in

1988 and for which he became recognized as a leading member of the avant-garde in China. An all-enveloping textual environment, *A Book from the Sky* is composed of massive sheets of Chinese characters, some left loose and some bound into books, which are suspended from the ceiling, pasted on the wall, and laid on the floor. Everything about *A Book from the Sky* has the look of authenticity. From its arrangement of headings and marginalia on the page to its string bindings and indigo covers, the work mimics in every detail the characteristics of traditional Chinese printing and book-making. While donning such a guise, however, *A Book from the Sky* is supremely inauthentic. Its characters are purely of the artist's invention and utterly without meaning. What is most unsettling perhaps is the way in which Xu Bing's characters approximate the real thing, for the artist has composed them from the variant parts that make up Chinese characters. In fact, Xu Bing's lexicon is derived from an authoritative Chinese dictionary, but subjected to a radically deconstructive *bricolage*.

Xu Bing
A Book from the Sky, 1987-1991
Installation view, Elvehjem Museum of Art,
University of Wisconsin-Madison

25

When it was initially shown in China, *A Book from the Sky* became the focus of instant acclaim and notoriety among artists and critics, provoking volumes of intense criticism. Some found the work a devastating critique of Chinese culture, a condemnation of its inutility and meaninglessness. Others viewed the work as a tribute to Chinese culture, a testament to the beauty and balance of its aesthetic structures as well as a distillation of the tenets of Chan Buddhism founded on a metaphysics of silence and paradox. The variety of opinions and the fervor of the discussions that greeted Xu Bing's work reflected the complex cultural conditions which gave rise to this ambitious project. In the eighties, with the demise of the Cultural Revolution and the onset of reform, China had entered into a new phase of critical introspection. The political policies of past years were opened to criticism, and the value of Marxist ideology itself reassessed. Chinese intellectuals feverishly argued over the solution to their country's problems, which were attributed not only to the disastrous effects of the Cultural Revolution but also to China's tardy or insufficient modernization. These discussions spread across different sectors, including artistic ones as well. Thus it was asked: What of the Chinese tradition should be discarded, utilized or reformed? What of the West should be adopted?

Xu Bing
A Book from the Sky, 1987-1991 (detail)

Regarded as an exemplary work of the period, Xu Bing's *A Book from the Sky* became a focal point for all the debates that revolved around the possible avenues of national and cultural reconstruction. But what the work does, in its highly ambivalent way, is to highlight such struggles and still refuse the possibility of any simple closure. While it speaks in a national syntax, it disarticulates such a syntax and renders it completely garbled. While it constructs a symbolic national text, it evacuates all meaning from such a text. In this way, the work calls attention to the ongoing crisis of modern China and at the same time calls into question any easy resolution of such a crisis which might be afforded by simple allegiance to culture and tradition. In *A Book from the Sky*, language—a symbolic system fundamental to the integrity and perpetuation of a national culture—is endlessly reproduced but vitiated of any functional value and thus made curiously unproductive.

With his latest work entitled *Tsan Series*, which was first shown in Boston in the fall of 1995, Xu Bing returns to similar concerns with the aid of some rather unusual artistic means—silkworms, or in Chinese "tsan,"[2] as invoked in the title of the piece. The *Tsan Series* is divided

2
The standard pinyin transliteration is "can." *Eds.*

into two parts. In the first, Xu Bing attaches silk moths to various papers and books bound in Western and Chinese styles. Organized into neat rows, the moths lay tiny eggs which compose the dot-like matrix of a "text" across the page. During the first month or so of the work's exhibition, the eggs hatch and baby silkworms emerge, thus constituting an ever-evolving type. For the second part of the *Tsan Series*, Xu Bing attaches silkworms as they reach

Xu Bing
Tsan Series—1, 1995
Silkworm eggs, mixed media
Installation view, Massachusetts College of Art, Boston

maturity for spinning silk to an assortment of objects, including a newspaper, a book on natural science, and a computer, among other things.
Settled into their new habitat, the silkworms begin to spin their silk,
enshrouding the objects in a gossamer web. Presented in vitrines like
carefully controlled science experiments, *Tsan Series* is a performative
installation that evolves through time.

If *A Book from the Sky* highlights the fate of a moribund culture, then
Tsan Series explores the possibilities of its re-propagation by presenting
an oddly arresting hybrid between nature and culture, the organic and
the inorganic. Natural reproduction and cultural production are here
layered on top of one another so that they become structurally one. As
Xu Bing explains, he was attracted to the way that silkworms work.
Slowly weaving back and forth in graceful, undulating movements, the
silkworms spit out an endless thread of silk until they exhaust themselves. As silkworms have long been harnessed for the creation of a
human material culture, cultivated for over four millennia, the endless
webs of silk spun in the *Tsan Series* become an embodiment of the persistence of culture itself.

As much as the *Tsan Series* is about procreativity, however, so is it
haunted by death. As much as it is about continuity, so is it haunted by
discontinuity. As the eggs hatch and the larvae roam across the page,
text is simultaneously composed and decomposed. They leave a trace,
but a trace that continually erases itself. The inevitable natural cycle
from life to death is in full evidence in the *Tsan Series*, where cocoons
are littered about like death shrouds. Like Xu Bing's *A Book from the
Sky*, his *Tsan Series* is a meditation on culture and knowledge, emphasiz-
ing here not so much the loss of meaning but the precariousness of its
making. The threads of silk in the *Tsan Series* thus become a poignant
metaphor for the fragile fabric from which a culture is woven, the spin-

ning of silk an allegory for the tenuous process of its production and reproduction.

Xu Bing
Tsan Series—2, 1995 (detail)
Live Silkworms, mixed media

For all of its skepticism about the efficacy and endurance of culture, Xu Bing's work is in the end striking in its stubborn dedication. Each of his projects has required herculean effort on the part of the artist. *A Book from the Sky*, for example, was the result of an intensive three-year period of labor, during which Xu Bing hand-carved the individual printing blocks for four thousand characters. The *Tsan Series*, in an equally taxing way, necessitated the breeding of five thousand silkworms for months in the artist's studio. Both of these projects are a testimony to the artist's tenacity, which offers a counterpoint to the work's seeming pessimism. Thus Xu Bing asks us: Can a culture rewrite itself through its own erasure? Can it reconstruct itself through its own unraveling?

1996

Interview with Hou Chun-ming[1]

1
This is one of three Chinese-language interviews which Alice Yang conducted in Taipei in January 1997 with artists participating in the exhibition, *Tracing Taiwan: Contemporary Works on Paper*, as part of the preparation for writing her essays for the exhibition catalogue of the same name. In the absence of those unwritten essays, the interviews were published in edited form in the catalogue, courtesy of the artists, Gerald Szeto, and the Yang family. The painstaking work of transcribing the interview tapes was undertaken by Chao-yi Tsai and Chang-Miao Huang, interns at the Chinese Information and Cultural Service, New York. The translation and editing of the transcripts was undertaken by Jonathan Hay. The interview text published here is a slightly abridged version of that published in the catalogue. *Eds.*

HCM: The highest ambition I have for my work is to achieve something like [the series] *Collecting Spirits* [1993]: a simple picture, with an image and an explanatory text (illustration on p. 127). I'm committed to a kind of work that involves commentary on the [image's] meaning. *Collecting Spirits* worked that way. [But] if you don't bring in depth, then all you have is a sign. Creating signs can be very satisfying. But you might want to develop things further—that's my present difficulty; the earlier things [now seem] too austere. . . . Formally, my system is chaotic. However, I use stylization to compensate for the weaknesses of this chaos. The kind of format that I used in [the series] *Erotic Paradise* [1992] and *Collecting Spirits*, for instance, allowed me to get the forms to settle down. [Individual] works like *Bastard and Bitch* or *The Divine Stick* [both 1996] can actually be seen as a kind of cartoon about current events, since they have both pictures and explanations. The content isn't all true, but I did use a current events approach to handle it.

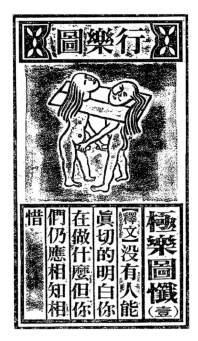

Hou Chun-ming
Work from *Erotic Paradise* series, 1992
Print
Series of eight works
41 x 31 1/2" each

The Divine Stick[2] reflects a series of recent religious incidents in Taiwan. In it you can see Taiwan's social problems and the phenomenon of people's anxiety. The religious craze among ordinary Taiwanese people has gone through one wave after another; moreover it has been [exploited] extremely efficiently and pragmatically. Taking advantage of people's faith, [religious leaders] raise money, with excellent results, so you get both financial and sexual exploitation, as happened in the incidents of fraud involving Sung Ch'i-li and Chan Master Miao-t'ien, for example. I'm fascinated by the power of control exercised over people by these prophets who are supposedly afflicted by their own desires, and who so cleverly transform desire into a kind of command.

AY: Let me ask you to speak about this series of works [*Bastard and Bitch*, *The Divine Stick*, *Coward*, *The Art of Body-Splitting*] as a group.
What the series explores is this: Why does desire become a source of difficulty? It's because it is normatized by society. In religious terms desires are a sin. There is satire in the works, but it is ambiguous and obscure; moreover, the criticism is many-sided. For example, in *The Divine Stick* I am satirizing the way religious leaders use the pretext of religion to exploit and control people, and even profit financially. I'm satirizing the way the believers, because of their stupidity, are manipulated. I satirize people who criticize this phenomenon, because a religious faith only exists if there are believers; without believers it wouldn't exist. If a believer has faith and is cured of an illness, this power is so authentic and massive that who are "outsiders" to repudiate it? The protagonists in the works include everybody involved; no one in particular is singled out. By ridiculing the incidents [of corruption], on the one hand I want to expose the problem, and on the other I want to eliminate it. To expose the problem is frightening, and to [aspire to] eliminate it is seemingly absurd. I don't establish a position, or follow any fixed principle; I hope that although I'm soft I have a certain

2
The term translated by the artist as "evangelist" is *shen-gun*, literally "divine stick." It refers to a false *tâng-ki*, or spirit medium: in other words, a religious charlatan. See David K. Jordan, *Gods, Ghosts, and Ancestors: The Folk Religion of a Taiwanese Village* (Berkeley: University of California Press, 1972), pp. 74-75.

toughness, but I waver. When you want to introduce social reforms, you have to put forward an ideal, but I don't have one; all I do is expose the embarrassment of the situation. When social reformers formulate their ideals of reform, their judgments of right and wrong are very clear, but later [their ideals] turn into another kind of oppression.

Some of your works bring together a lot of different ideas; they seem to be critiquing certain social phenomena, but also to be private discoveries and explorations. In the West, artistic critique [often] takes up the viewpoint of an observer. What is your position?
I pay equal attention to the personal and the public. It's a special characteristic of creative work that there is a constant to-and-fro between them. For example, if an issue is my personal concern as an individual, I may find some social phenomenon that I can attach it to and project it onto. I transform my own concern into a social one. Or a social issue may provide me with a subject or an inspiration which I turn into a personal concern in the course of expressing it. People who criticize my work usually see it too simplistically; I see it as complex, because there are so many twists and turns.

There is no right or wrong in your paintings, no morality, no difference between good and bad; this might be said to be a representation of Taiwanese society. Does your art have this kind of outlook or not?
Taiwan's "chaotic disorder" that people often speak of is in my opinion usually just a cliché. People in any period may arrive at the conclusion that their own period is the most chaotic, but judging by what I have seen in my travels, it's true that Taiwan is relatively dirty and chaotic, and not very law-abiding.

Does your work have a political viewpoint?
It isn't a very clear one. For example, I am a so-called homeland

[*bentu*] artist, but if you compare it with the way the Democratic Progress Party is actively exploiting [the idea of] homeland culture in order to build up its political capital, my homeland is something I can't do anything about, but is the origin of all my experiences and creative work. If I'm an honest person, and sensitive to my surroundings, then the things I express will of course have a homeland character.

The relation of your work to folk art, folk rituals?
. . . Around four or five years ago, whenever there was a temple festival or some special ritual I would immediately want to go and observe it. As soon as I heard the sound of those drums I would get excited. That lasted for over a year, during which I regularly participated in the rituals. For example, one year on a Buddhist festival day, I rode a motorcycle along the main streets, and on the street and in the lanes every house was burning gold paper, one brazier for every household. I remember thinking that if I could have floated in the air and looked down over Taiwan, then it would have been one great sea of fire. That was a really superb kind of performance art; I hope to be able to create similar rituals. This kind of religious faith which is so deeply rooted in people's hearts has really massive power; it's also a very positive resource.

Since the lifting of martial law [1987], has there been more interest in Taiwan in popular culture?
Yes. But when I was dealing with popular culture, the interest hadn't taken off yet. While I was doing my investigation in the south, it was from the standpoint of an observer and an educated person. Then one morning I found myself back in the city, and I was like a person from the south, I wasn't urbanized enough. There was a kind of disruption of my social identity. . . . Since the lifting of martial law, Minnan[3] popular culture has attracted attention, and because of the disruption I myself felt, I'm convinced that it can be a stimulus for creative work.

3
Minnan, literally "southern Min," refers to the southern province of present-day Fujian province in China, of which Taiwan was once a part and with which it shares many cultural continuities.

33

Translation: It was the eighty-fifth year of the Republic [1996]. The weather was sweltering hot, and people's morality was not what it used to be. A man and a woman were overjoyed to be in love and could not restrain themselves from being affectionate. They regretted they couldn't be like birds or beasts, fondling and mating any time, any place. One day they disguised themselves as wild dogs and openly had sex on the street. They felt no shame at all. But while they were carried away an enraged officer of the law beat them to death with a stick. Documented by Mr. Hou of Liujiao in the *bingzi* year [1996].

Hou Chun-ming
Bastard and Bitch, 1996
Print
75 1/8 x 86 1/4"

Translation: It was the eighty-fifth year of the Republic [1996]. The weather was sweltering hot, and people's morality was not what it used to be. There was a prophet who suffered from a constant erection, so he castrated himself. But the penis still maintained its erection as if it was still a living thing. He took the religious name of Divine Stick. When he placed the penis in the lower body of his followers, suddenly Heaven merged with the human. If they held it in their arms, then all their worries dissolved. Only the intellectuals, without sincerity or sensitivity, considered it a hoax. He was arrested and found guilty. Documented by Mr. Hou of Liujiao in the *bingzi* year [1996].

Hou Chun-ming
The Divine Stick, 1996
Print
75 1/8 x 86 1/4"

Hou Chun-ming
Coward, 1996
Print
75 1/8 x 86 1/4"

Translation: It was the eighty-fifth year of the Republic [1996]. The weather was sweltering hot, and people's morality was not what it used to be. There was a young man who was frustrated at work and craved love and caresses. Skipping work, he went to look for his mother. She was taking a bath, so he dived into the water and squeezed himself back into his mother's body. Within her uterus, enveloped in placenta and floating in the fluid, his happiness knew no bounds. He was reluctant to leave. But one day his father returned. His enormous penis penetrated Mother's womb. With no place to hide, the son was battered to death. Documented by Mr. Hou of Liujiao in the *bingzi* year [1996].

Hou Chun-ming
The Art of Body-Splitting, 1996
Print
75 1/8 x 86 1/4"

Translation: It was the eighty-fifth year of the Republic [1996]. The weather was sweltering hot, and people's morality was not what it used to be. There was a young man who wanted to have sex with two lovers simultaneously. But no matter what, he always lost sight of one while attending to the other, so that whatever he did he always ended up being blamed. He was often on the verge of being torn apart. But after suffering these torments for a long time, he transcended them and mastered the art of body-splitting. Thereafter he was able to follow his desires. He could take back or give out his dismembered body as he pleased. He let his jealous and resentful lovers rip him apart and felt no pain. Documented by Mr. Hou of Liujiao in the *bingzi* year [1996].

35

Is there any change in your approach nowadays compared with four or five years ago?

Now I almost never go to see folk rituals. If I were to do any more work related to them, then I would hope to be able to spend time living in that cultural context, and not just be a tourist who only turns up when there's a festival.

Folk customs and folk rituals in Taiwan are in transformation overall. In your work, there are [also elements of] mass culture, by which I mean [cultural elements] that have only come into being under modern capitalism. Your work combines these two distinctive features at least.

You could say that my creative work opts for the "low." This "low" character takes form through fiercely flowing desires, and I worry a lot that other people will misunderstand my work. There are people who criticize my work as being too direct, too explicit, [but] from my point of view this is not a negative judgment. It's an understanding of things that I'm after. An artist shouldn't be elitist and cut himself off from the population at large. If someone criticizes a particular work on non-artistic grounds, always assuming that the person is interested in the questions raised by the work, then I'm delighted.

So that's why you've exhibited your work in the street in the past. Along different lines, I'd like to come back to the question of popular Buddhist and Taoist rituals in Taiwan. Taiwanese religious rituals commonly involve the human body, are extremely primitive, and are generally lower-class, in contrast to the way the role of the body is played down in Euro-American religion. Taking the *tâng-ki*[4] as an example, perhaps it is because of rural society that the religious ritual takes form through the body and its desires.

Some *tâng-ki* prove their piety and abilities through self-mutilation. For

4
The *tâng-ki* is a medium, of whom a spirit takes possession. The *tâng-ki* plays an important role in the community, as one of the principal means by which divination is carried out. For an anthropological account, see Jordan (1972), pp. 67-86.

the *tâng-ki*, the use of a knife or a stick to hurt oneself has two purposes: first, he wants to demonstrate his piety through the pain he
feels when he hurts himself; but for most people, a demonstration like
the *tâng-ki*'s is something they couldn't go through themselves, so that
it also demonstrates his special capacities. The blood-letting establishes
an effect of power. If my work has such a strong narrative character, it's
a development of the underside of modern art. To me, modern art has
too much fear of getting dirty; it's too concerned with purity. Although
modern art has managed to gain its autonomy from politics and religion
with great difficulty, it has been at the price of suppressing the relation
between people and society. To most people, elements of story-telling
are very attractive, and in the process an interaction is produced. I
don't mind if people say my work is didactic, since this is something I
want. What I care more about is whether this didacticism has a degree
of richness itself. For example, there's a requirement in traditional
[Chinese] art of "a narrow channel of water flowing over a long distance." There can't be any anger, it has to be mild and smooth, and
rounded out; if a glance is enough to grasp the meaning then it goes
against tradition, because the work can't sustain reflection. In Chinese
terms, "high-quality" art has to be able to stimulate reflection, though
under these constraints many things are lost. [In traditional Chinese
art] a transcendence of the moment is what the artist is seeking in the
work. The requirement I have of my own work is not that. Even if the
work gets just a moment of attention, or a laugh, this is still worth
having. I approve of works which go in the direction of explosiveness;
their power is something which those other works certainly can't replace.

**Still, these two things are not in conflict or in opposition. If you can
grasp the truth of a period, then [the work] transcends its moment.
. . . If you were [deliberately] to pursue a transcendence of the
moment, then it would become extremely abstract, and unfathomable.**

I hope to keep hold of one principle in my creative work, which is that I have to be able to resolve issues that are my own. And because my art is about resolving my personal issues, these works all have a certain ritual meaning.

Could you speak, as someone of your generation of young Taiwanese artists, about the complex relation between the sexes in Taiwan?
The respective positions, statuses, and obligations [of men and women] are all in disorder, but from an artist's point of view this disorder is beneficial. When everything's too orderly it's bad for art. Ultimately the criterion of value of artistic creation is its ability to break with convention and create something vital. As an artist, though it may be profiting from the misfortune of others or fishing in troubled waters, I'm able to do creative work in this situation of disorder. It's a very lively environment. What I call disorder is where things haven't yet been settled; when one day they get settled, conversely creativity declines. Disorder and vitality are symbiotically linked. I have a positive opinion of the disorder.

On the issue of sexual equality, how have Taiwanese intellectuals reacted to your work?
Feminists regularly criticize my work as male-chauvinist. I do see the world from a male point of view, and my work in the end reveals a male outlook, since that represents my own gender experience; moreover, I certainly don't shrink from becoming an object of attack.

This series of works—*The Art of Body-Splitting*, *The Divine Stick*, and so on—might be said to depict the failure of male-chauvinism.
Speaking as a man, we're going through a difficult period. Women, legally and institutionally, have certainly received unfair treatment. But in terms of ordinary living, they may be more powerful than men.

Contemporary culture molds men to be oppressors, but all our social resources go to support women. I don't appreciate arguments that turn male and female positions into a confrontation. All people, events, and things should be approached on the basis of mutual benefit and concern.

When one looks at your work at first, it seems extremely physical, with a tendency to aggression, very much in a male mode. But looking at it more closely, there is great ambiguity.
To take *The Art of Body-Splitting* as an example, I've already changed the text once: the first text I printed talked about how the man was torn apart by two women, but later I changed this to be the result of his own wish. I've always been careful to avoid falling into the trap of separating men and women into oppressors and oppressed.

When I raised the question of political ideals earlier, it was because I was thinking about a relationship between *The Art of Body-Splitting* and the Taiwanese political situation, given that Taiwan's situation of political impotence is quite consistent with your work.
The Art of Body-Splitting and *The Divine Stick* are both [related to] this kind of situation.

Why is desire an important theme for you at the moment?
To answer that, I have to go back to what we were just talking about, the situation following the lifting of martial law. When political pressure was intense, people's desires were suppressed. Conversely, when political control was relaxed, people's characters and desires surfaced strongly. One could say that on a social level . . . my age-group with its particular desires is going through a difficult period, in line with our circumstances; I have to articulate this through my art. The works may seem to be attacking others, but they are actually an attack on myself. I'm someone with a very strong sense of morality. Some people think

my work puts morality in danger, that it's an attempt to subvert social order, but this is just the most superficially accessible aspect of the work. In fact, its main objective is to find a solution to my inner conflicts. Earlier Taiwanese artists kept a distance between the artist and the artwork, even hiding themselves behind the artwork; I don't do that, I put myself right in front. Speaking as an artist, I want to exploit my own experience in order to make a contribution to society. Although most of my works are depictions of failure, still the [act of] depiction itself is a contribution. This point of view has been stimulated by what I've learned from the experience of feminists; the only difference [between my position and theirs] is one of role and vantage point.

1997

Reviews

On Kawara

The unique format for this exhibition at the Dia Center for the Arts has been astutely conceived as a foil for the work of On Kawara, a conceptual artist who has been widely acclaimed since the 1970s.[1] Taking place over the period of one year, the length of all exhibitions at this non-profit art space, the installation is comprised of three parts: the text work *One Million Years (Past)*, the sound piece *One Million Years (Future)*, and a changing selection from the *Today Series* each month. Pristine in its presentation and rigorous in structure, this exhibition is spare almost to the point of monotony and yet highly resonant in the ways in which it orchestrates the inter-relationships between three projects and foregrounds Kawara's central concerns with temporal progression and change.

1
Originally on view at Dia Center for the Arts, January 1 - December 31, 1993. *Eds.*

The centerpiece of this installation, the *Today Series*, is an ongoing painting project which Kawara began in 1966. Each painting simply records the date of its execution in white letters and numerals on a monochrome background. In keeping with this conceptual concision, Kawara has restricted his project to four standard canvas sizes and a handful of background colors—grey, blue, orange, red. When not on display, each painting is stored in a cardboard box, along with a clipping from a local newspaper of the same date as the painting. For the Dia installation, Kawara has chosen to display all the paintings executed since 1966 in New York. Each month finds a different segment of the project, with a selection of chronologically sequential paintings. The bland reiteration of the project speaks to the repetitive nature of daily existence. But amidst this unending pattern, subtle variations begin to emerge. An expanse of grey painting gives way to a brilliant patch of orange reds; a row of small canvases are suddenly punctuated by a large

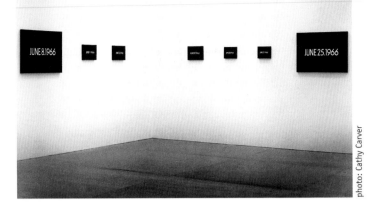

photo: Cathy Carver

On Kawara
One Thousand Days One Million Years, January 1 - December 31, 1993
Installation view, Dia Center for the Arts, New York

one. Order and randomness play against one another. A display of some of the painting boxes with their newspaper headlines recalls cataclysmic events that once transpired—the hostage crisis in Iran, the Nicaraguan revolution. The *Today Series* subtly turns our attention to the drama and meaning buried in the monotony of the everyday.

The quotidian marked by the *Today Series* contrasts with the much larger sequence of time recorded by the two other projects. *One Million Years (Past)* is a ten-volume epic that lists, page after page, each of the preceding one million years. *One Million Years (Future)* is an audio piece which counts, year after year, in the opposite direction. Together, the three projects set up a dialogue between past, present, and future, between the individual and the collective, specificity and anonymity. Providing an unusual opportunity to see the *Today Series* in an extensive sequence, this installation attests to the monumental accretion of Kawara's disciplined daily practice and prompts a moment of meditation in the headlong rush of time.

1993

Long Chin-san

The impact of the West on the development of modern Chinese art is a subject that has yet to receive thorough critical coverage. *Painterly Images*[1] provided a rare glimpse into this history as embodied in the work of Long Chin-san, a remarkable 101-year-old whose career coincided with a century of tumultuous changes in Chinese culture. Born in Zhejiang province in 1892 and a longtime resident of Taiwan, Long is a pioneer of art photography in China. In adopting a modern technology imported initially from the West, he thus confronted one of the issues most hotly debated among his contemporaries. It is telling that Long sought not to emulate any Western styles or genres but to reconcile photography with the tradition of Chinese aesthetics. Like many of his generation in artistic as well as political and social arenas, he tried to harness technology for the preservation of Chinese culture. The results are extremely revealing about the historical encounter between China and the West and compelling in their own right.

1
Originally on view at Taipei Gallery, New York, August 13 - September 17, 1993. *Eds.*

The photographs included in *Painterly Images* span the 1930s through the 1970s. Most take the form of Long's signature "composite pictures" which collage together images from different sources to create facsimiles of Chinese landscape painting. In them, Long

Long Chin-san
Sailing Through the Gorge, 1985
Composite photograph
16 1/2 x 11 1/2"
Courtesy Taipei Gallery, New York

45

rehearses a repertoire of motifs—a pagoda nestled in the mountains, fishermen rowing boats, cranes beneath pine trees—along with compositional trademarks of Chinese painting tradition. These monochromatic photographs have a dreamy ethereality that seems initially at odds with traces of their photographic realism. Through this peculiar conjunction of the imaginary and the factual, however, Long's work yields keen insights into two seemingly disparate modes. Recapturing painterly conventions from bygone times through the documentary lens of photography, Long's work brings into relief the idealized nature of Chinese landscape painting and in turn revives the lyricism of a practice that has often fallen into rote use. In a parallel fashion, Long's work also reveals photography's artful artifice, at a time when many still cling to the true value of photography.

Long's works are thus most successful when they emphasize their own fictive character. In one work, for example, he foregoes real-life models completely and photographs a small replica of a thatch-roofed hut with a few twigs as substitutes for trees, creating a charming, miniature world. In contrast, his large-scale photographs, which collage figures together with landscape elements seamlessly, veer towards a kind of literalism that collapses the arresting tensions possible in his work. At his best, Long combines painterly and photographic languages together in a new, critical inflection. He suggests how the interaction between technology and traditional Chinese aesthetic principles need not lead to the eclipse of one by the other but can result in the innovation of both.

1993

Bing Lee

Bing Lee's recent show was an imaginative foray into chance operation, the results of which were elegant and playful at the same time.[1] The exhibition's structure was pre-determined yet embraced the possibility for change and improvisation. Its centerpiece was a wall of drawings, on which images accrued over the course of the exhibition. Starting with a blank wall, Lee added to it each day, putting up one or sometimes two to three drawings which he had completed the previous night. The extension of the drawings into space and their growing articulation of meaning was akin to the transformation and sedimentation of organic processes.

Like the exhibition format, each image on the wall was also in itself free-form, resulting from Lee's unexpected fusion of different shades and motifs—a leg in high-heel shoe sprouting from two ovals; a wafer-patterned cigar pierced through a boat; two knives propped up against each other to form the Chinese character for "man." Many of these images incorporate elements, like the recurrent motif of two interlocking circles, that recall Chinese ideograms and folk art traditions. Despite their curious mutation, the images have an internal logic bound by the fluidity of Lee's draughtsmanship. Together, they conjure up a polymorphous and polyglot universe, where the organic meets up with the geometric, the industrial with the folk, East with West. Encoding the workings of a protean imagination, they invite attempts at decoding to fulfill the promise of embedded meanings.

The images shown at this exhibition are derived from a long-time practice by this New York-based artist, originally from Hong Kong. For over ten years, Lee has been maintaining a pictodiary, a daily log of

1
Originally on view at East West Cultural Studies, New York, January 11-29, 1994. *Eds.*

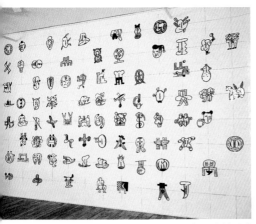

Bing Lee
You Have The Right To (Chant, But) Remain Silent, 1994
Installation view, East West Cultural Center, New York
Acrylic, epoxy, chalk, and paper on wall
Series of eighty-seven works
12 x 12" each

pictorial forms. Each night, sitting down with a sheet of rice paper, Lee registers the random images which float spontaneously into consciousness. Although his procedure bears some resemblance to Surrealist automatism, it is linked also to Eastern meditative practices, in which the mind is emptied out. As a child, Lee was taught to meditate by his uncle, who had an avid interest in Buddhism. Lee's own engagement with religion has been deepened by recent visits to Tibet and the Dunhuang caves in China.

The Buddhist dimension was especially pronounced in this exhibition. To each image on the central wall, Lee has added an incantation that begins with *a-mi-to-fo*, or "Amitabha" Buddha. Two other parts of the exhibition extended this religious framework. On one wall, Lee displayed three large canvases dotted by rows of circles; on another was a series of thirty-six smaller canvases in which the pictodiary images were superimposed on top of a field of circles. The repetitive grid of circles is a feature borrowed also from Buddhist practice. Monks use the marking of circles as a notational device in meditation, with one circle denoting the completion of one chant. The chants are repeated until the page is filled. Combined, the three parts of Lee's exhibition presented an eloquent rumination on the integral relationship between improvisation and discipline, mystery and clarity, flux and order.

1994

Ping Chong

"Whose history is this anyway?" This is the refrain which threads
through Ping Chong's *Chinoiserie*, a multimedia theater piece that
explores the fateful origins and discordant developments of the Sino-
Western encounter.[1] The question is clearly a rhetorical one. History is
not the sole province of any one protagonist, but is played out in the
collision between competing forces and perspectives. Such is the case of
China's relation to the West, which has long been mired in misunder-
standing and hostility. But as Ping Chong points out mid-way through
the performance: "History is written by the victors, you know." While
sensitive to the prevalence of prejudice across different cultures,
Chinoiserie is a bitter rumination on a lopsided exchange of power, in
which China has so often lost its self-determination and its people
suffered the persistent effects of discrimination and mistrust.

To recount this complex history, Chong adopts a multilinear narrative
that cuts back and forth between past and present, between official
and personal history, between recorded events and private anecdotes.
Assisted by a cast of four multiracial performers, Ping Chong stands at a
bright red lectern like a master of ceremonies and narrates the elaborate proceedings. Fast-dissolving slide projections and an atmospheric
musical score are combined with snippets of song, dance movement and
dialogue to create this densely woven ninety-minute-long montage.

Among its many themes, *Chinoiserie* focuses on two in particular. It
begins with the meeting in 1793 between the British Ambassador Lord
McCartney and China's Emperor Qianlong. A trade emissary from King
George III, McCartney's mission was motivated by Britain's ever-growing
ambitions in the world market. While hoping to gain new ports in China

1
Originally performed at the
Next Wave Festival, Brooklyn
Academy of Music, Majestic
Theater, November 14-18,
1995. *Eds.*

photo: Carol Rosegg

Ping Chong and Company
Chinoiserie, 1995
Brooklyn Academy of Music, Next Wave Festival
Foreground: Shi-Zheng Chen
Background: Ping Chong

and to secure a relaxation of trade restrictions, McCartney and his party refused to submit to Chinese demands and execute the ritual kowtow to their Celestial Emperor. *Chinoiserie* enacts this symbolic struggle through a series of vignettes that capture, with increasing tension, the mutual distrust and confrontational stance between two sovereign powers. "Boom, boom, boom," the chorus chants, signaling ominously the repercussions of this first encounter, as Britain and other European powers eventually forced their entry into a recalcitrant China.

The other focal point of *Chinoiserie* reveals the Chinese American perspective from which Chong reviews the legacy of Sino-Western relations. It centers on the story of Vincent Chin, a young Chinese American who was beaten to death in 1982 by a Detroit auto worker and his stepson. Mistaken for a Japanese, Chin was a victim of the mounting frustrations of the American auto industry which found blame for its decline in Japan. Chin's murder, pivotal in the raising of Chinese American race consciousness, is told from the viewpoint of his mother who remembers him as both "a good Chinese" and "a good American." This observation, delivered with pathos and sorrow, points to the seemingly irreparable fracture lines in present-day race relations. As a Chinese American himself, Ping Chong has experienced first-hand the effects of such divisiveness. Throughout, he relays instances of both subtle and overt racial stereotyping he has endured, giving *Chinoiserie* a sense of real-life immediacy.

The high seriousness of the themes explored in *Chinoiserie* is often belied by the production's irreverent sense of humor. Describing the growing tensions generated by Lord McCartney's trip, one actor exclaims: "They went ape-shit chow-mein." As he has done since the 1970s, this well-regarded director and performance artist draws freely from what seems like an encyclopedic knowledge of pop culture. Part Brechtian theater and part cocktail lounge act, *Chinoiserie* offers musical fragments of Broadway show tunes as well as the 1970s disco hit "Kung Fu Fighting." It also borrows liberally from Chinese opera and martial arts for its stylized choreography. Added to this mix is a kaleidoscopic slide show of archival images from the nineteenth and twentieth centuries which illustrate, among other things, Europe's obsession with tea, opium dens, Chong's Chinatown boyhood, and the building of the transcontinental railroad by Chinese laborers.

It is not easy to hold all of these pieces together. Layered one on top of another, the surfeit of images and texts can be at times exhilarating and at times laborious. After a while, all the kitschy asides become so many nervous flourishes which detract from the production's dramatic arc. The abrupt shifts in tone and viewpoint also have mixed results for the telling of history. At its best, *Chinoiserie* brings the past and its conflicting vantage points vibrantly to life. At its least effective, it collapses complex historical events into flip one-liners that verge on the cliché.

Still, *Chinoiserie* has a number of arresting and moving moments, orchestrated with a finesse that makes their final impact all the more surprising. Throughout *Chinoiserie*, for example, Chong makes reference to America's favorite pastime, baseball. At several points, this national mythology is evoked aurally through the familiar crack of a bat hitting a ball. A rousing duet of "Take Me Out to the Ball Game" is sung in

English and Chinese, giving a new multicultural twist to this American anthem. Only after all these sounds and motifs have accumulated does Chong reveal that Vincent Chin was beaten to death with a baseball bat. With this devastating revelation, Chong gives a stinging critique of racism and its tragic consequences.

1996

photo: Carol Rosegg

Ping Chong and Company
Chinoiserie, 1995
Brooklyn Academy of Music, Next Wave Festival
Foreground: Shi-Zheng Chen

Sowon Kwon's Interior Schemes

"Dear, dear! How queer everything is today!" So Alice exclaimed when she ventured into a topsy-turvy Wonderland. Like Lewis Carroll's heroine, visitors to Sowon Kwon's exhibition *Interior Schemes* encounter everyday surroundings made strangely unfamiliar.[1] Just as Alice found her body changing abruptly in size, so proportions here are askew and perspectives off-kilter. The focal point of Kwon's mixed-media exhibition is the domestic interior. Adapting its various architectural and spatial features to her own "design," Kwon explores the dense cultural meanings attached to this site. While the interior is typically associated with comfort and stability, what results in Kwon's work is a place where things and bodies no longer feel at home.

1
Originally on view at Lombard-Freid Fine Arts, New York, February 23 - March 30, 1996. *Eds.*

A tour of this space might begin with *The Master's Drawing Room*, which commands the central wall of Kwon's exhibition. A two-dimensional wall relief, *The Master's Drawing Room* is made up of schematic representations of assorted furnishings—a child's bed, a drawing room table, a fireplace, a sofa—each of which is rendered according to a different perspectival standard. Kwon's meticulous mapping of perspectives is tantalizing, enticing the viewer's attempt at

All photos courtesy Lombard/Fried Fine Arts, New York

Sowon Kwon
The Master's Drawing Room, 1996
Wood, paint, plaster
Dimensions variable

53

spatial resolution and so imaginary entry into the room. Yet although we move around to find a point of spatial stability, things never fall into place. The sofa, modeled after the Anglo-Japanese furniture produced by the Victorian designer E.W. Godwin, is so elongated in perspective that it seems irrevocably distorted. In other words, *The Master's Drawing Room* does not cohere. Its coordinates remain altogether unstable.

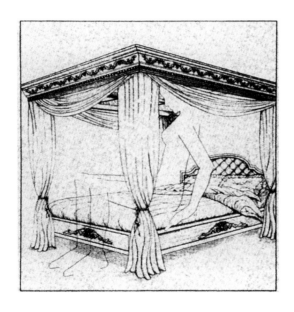

Sowon Kwon
Average Female(1), 1995
Blueprint
18 x 24"

Kwon depicts the incompatibility of bodies with space in more tangible ways in her *Average Female* series. These ethereal blueprints draw upon two conventions: ergonomic templates of the female body used by industrial designers, and models of rococo-ish interiors found in architectural catalogues. The interior, traditionally viewed as the space of feminine domesticity, is decorated here with a "feminine" touch in all of its fussy ornamental details. Yet female body and interior are graphed together in ways that are strikingly at odds with each other. The figures, much too large in scale, are crammed into stairwells and canopied beds, just like the illustrations of Alice stuck in the rooms of Wonder-

land. Perverting the logic of ergonomics, Kwon reveals the interior as a
space of the body's regulation and confinement.

In two other works in the exhibition, Kwon transforms the interior from
a place of rigid containment to one of fluid infiltration. *Wainscot
(Bosses)* is a fleshly remake of a familiar architectural detail. The units
of this wainscoting are composed of wood and a series of computer-
generated photographs of skin. Highly abstracted, the images of the
skin take on the fine pattern and delicate color of decorator's fabric.
Molding (Smoke Stain Rose) con-
sists of plaster units, decorated
with repetitive motifs, which are
installed just slightly above eye
level. Upon closer examination,
the rosy protrusions that adorn
this molding turn out to be
nipple casts. Like Jean Cocteau's
anthropomorphic candelabras in
his film *Beauty and the Beast*,
both works are haunting
presences in Kwon's interior, their
peculiar viscerality embodying the
return of the repressed.

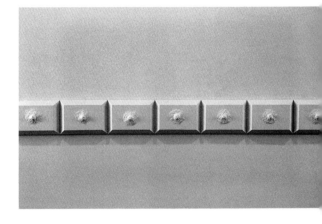

Sowon Kwon
Molding (smoke stain rose), 1996 (detail)
Plaster, paint
2 1/2 x 35 x 1" per block of 10

Kwon, a Korean American artist
born in Seoul in 1963, brings
several lines of inquiry together in her densely packed work—from the
nexus between interiority and femininity, to the history of the private
interior as the privileged precinct of the modern bourgeois subject, and
the confluence between interior decoration and Orientalism as exemplified by the work of E.W. Godwin. From these and other vantage points,

Kwon calls into question the normative standards that shape our experience of the interior. Kwon's exhibition is distinguished not only by its intellectual breadth but also by its visual eloquence. Each work in *Interior Schemes* supplements and amplifies the other, thus evoking the interior's multiple resonances as well as reinvesting it with new, unexpected psychic valency. Engaging the viewer in reconsiderations of body and space, culture and design, in physically palpable and conceptually provocative ways, Kwon has created a fresh approach to the genre of "site-specific" work.

1996

Chen Zhen

Chen Zhen's *Daily Incantations* is a work of highly singular means.[1] For this sculptural installation, Chen gathered from China 101 wooden chamber pots. Suspended from tiered racks, these lowly objects of daily use are wrought into a surprisingly stately structure. Their arrangement is modeled after that of chime-bells, an ancient musical instrument produced thousands of years ago in Bronze Age China. In the center of this structure, Chen inserted another edifice—a large satellite-like globe composed of television sets, computers, radios, and other used electronic goods. The result is a striking work of stark contrasts, setting bodily waste against consumer refuse, the man-made against the industrial, the ancient against the modern.

1
Originally on view at Deitch Projects, New York, May 4 – June 8, 1996. *Eds.*

Chen Zhen
Daily Incantations, 1996
Installation view, Deitch Projects, New York
Courtesy Deitch Projects, New York

Chen's juxtapositions set up a series of reverberating riffs. The works register, first and foremost, the relationship between the industrialized West and the developing country that is China. For Chen, a Chinese artist based in Paris, life in China is represented by the chamber pots. A soundtrack of brushes vigorously scrubbing and water swooshing accompanies the installation, evoking the morning ritual of cleaning the pots familiar from Chen's childhood. Once prevalent in China, chamber pots are becoming increasingly obsolete with the country's swift industrialization and market transformation, particularly evident in the artist's native Shanghai. And Chen identifies these inevitable forces of change as Western—a culture of capitalism that spreads its reach through the mass of electronic gadgetry and communications equipment assembled at the installation's center. Chen's project also makes reference, albeit more obliquely, to other everyday rituals once common in China. Mixed into the work's soundtrack is a recording of people reading from Mao's *Little Red Book*, a daily communal rite enforced in schools and work units during the heyday of Mao's regime.

These daily incantations, as Chen has explained, were meant to "cleanse the soul." Pairing this allusion with the hygienic uses of the chamber pots, Chen seems to make subtle mockery of the Communist system of political indoctrination, inculcated under the name of spiritual purification. It is interesting to note here that Communist leaders also adapted ancient chime-bells to ideological ends, mounting rousing performances of Communist anthems, such as *The East is Red*, on famous sets of ancient bells. On one level, then, Chen's transformation of chamber pots into chime-bells seems also to satirize the grandiose display of power that is at a far remove from the necessities of everyday life.

Ultimately, however, Chen's verdict on China's past and present fate seems ambiguous. If the artist intends a critique, he also seems nostalgic about a bygone way of life, fast disappearing under the impact of Western-style capitalism. The work's Chinese title provides some clues, perhaps, to these ambivalences. The word *zhou*, translated here as "incantations," has both negative and positive connotations. While it refers to the weaving of spells and verbal charms, it can also mean the swearing of a deadly curse. On this dual register, then, Chen's *Daily Incantations* may be understood as both an exorcism and an invocation reflecting the complex process of negotiating China's past and future.

Incantations have a spiritual function as part of magic rituals, and this adds another important dimension to Chen's work. In ancient China, chime-bells were used most often during ancestral rites, to entertain the heavenly guests and thus to obtain their blessings. Chen's interest in rituals points to a broad metaphysical strain in his work. What is ultimately at issue in Chen's work, it seems, is the question of change and transformation fundamental to Chinese metaphysics. The found objects in this installation bear the trace and patina of time, whether they be outmoded industrial debris or the dilapidated containers of organic waste, with their chipped paint and cracked veneers. Pairing these two categories of objects, Chen's installation exposes the endless cycle of consumption and reproduction that ultimately transcends the economic and political fortunes of any one nation. In Daily Incantations, Chen Zhen offers us an eloquent meditation on everyday life, its constant mutability and its eternal rhythms.

1996

A Group Show: "We Are The Universe"

In the past few years, Asian American artists and curators have begun
to function more and more as a distinct community, forging ties
through conferences, exhibitions, and other group activities. *We Are The
Universe* signals the development of this trend even within the commer-
cial art world.[1] In the manner of a compendium or digest, it brought
together eleven artists of Asian background based in the U.S. (The
gallery is run by Kangki and Kangja Lee, who are originally from Korea.)
In spite of its grandiloquent title, the exhibition did not advance a
grandiose or unified Asian American vision. Instead, it opted for variety
in styles and media. The installations yielded some awkward juxtapositions that did not always serve the artists on display. A few of the works
also seemed rather hackneyed in concept, though polished in technical
execution. Nonetheless, exhibitions of this kind are thought-provoking
and fulfill an important purpose, especially in giving exposure to
mid-career artists who are often neglected in favor of either more
established or newer voices.

Although variety was stressed, a few themes did emerge. The prominence of abstract and figurative painting, whose fortunes have been
rocky of late in the U.S., was especially striking. Each season seems to
bring new attempts to resuscitate painting, only to have it fall from
favor again. *We Are The Universe* confirmed the persistence of the
medium among artists, despite quibbles among critics. An assortment
of approaches to painting was in evidence.

Helen Oji's bold contours and Hei Myung Hyun's decorative patterns
share an affinity for the graphic arts, while Jenny Chen's paintings
rework the language of gestural abstraction. Colin Lee and Younhee

1
Originally on view at Haenah-
Kent Gallery, New York,
December 11, 1993 - January
8, 1994. *Eds.*

60

Reviews

Paik command a virtuoso technique well suited to large-scale compositions. In Lee's case, this is combined with a distinctive palette of dense,
subtle hues. Lee's paintings, depicting chairs and organic forms, are
hard to pinpoint in terms of content. Still, they have a moodiness and
enigmatic quality that is highly evocative.

While these approaches are
not uncommon to the
repertory of Western con-
temporary art, other artists
in the exhibition seek
themes and images more
specific to the Asian experience. Zhang Hongtu, for
example, has adopted Mao
Zedong as the leitmotif of
his works for the last few
years. Mao's head is ren-
dered always as a cut-out,
leaving a ghostly yet unmis-
takably iconic presence.
Zhang's latest works have
the veiled liquidity of
Chinese ink washes but are

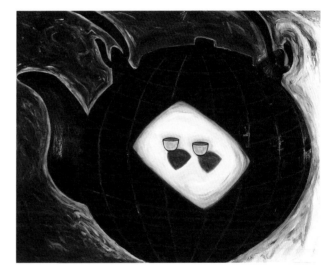

Helen Oji
Negotiation, 1991
Oil on canvas
60 x 72"

done in a novel medium—soy sauce. In this, Zhang has found a surprisingly flexible and lush material that also implies, in combination with
Mao's image, an ironic opposition between political ideology and daily
necessity, high and low.

Lynne Yamamoto explores a more personal and feminine terrain, reflected in the miniature scale of her sculptural work. Her exquisite pieces,

61

fashioned out of glass vessels and rusted metal, suggest the accretion of time and the condensation of memory. They pay tribute to the labor and struggles of her grandmother's immigrant experience.

Bing Lee's paintings are composed of a unique symbolic language that fuses motifs from East and West, the industrial and the organic, the modern and the folk. The protean mutability of Lee's ideograms encodes processes of invention and transformation—an apt metaphor for the Asian American experience as a whole.

1994

Zhang Hongtu
Mao—The Drawing #6, 1993
Soy sauce on rice paper, mounted on pages of the
Little Red Book, sealed by epoxy resin
28 x 20"

Looking for the Identity of Korean Art

For observers and critics of Asian American culture, this was what could
be considered a boon year in New York. The opening of *Across the Pacific:
Contemporary Korean and Korean American Art* at the Queens Museum last
October marked the beginning of an unusually active season in the field
of Asian American art.[1] In quick succession, the exhibition was followed
by two other milestone events: *Beyond Boundaries*, the first national
conference dedicated to Asian American visual, media, and performing
arts, in December,[2] and *Asia/America: Identities in Asian American Art*,
an exhibition that is slated for an extensive tour through other U.S.
cities after its run at New York's Asia Society this spring.[3]

Curiously, these events within the realm of high art coincided also with
a period of high visibility for Asian American themes in mass culture.
Two films exploring inter-generational relationships among Chinese
American immigrants and families—*The Joy Luck Club* and *The Wedding
Banquet*—enjoyed extensive runs in U.S. movie theaters in late 1993
and attracted considerable press interest. Whether in the form of a
critical inquiry geared towards art audiences or metamorphosed as a
Hollywood melodrama aimed at mass appeal, this flurry of activities
reflects the accelerated growth of the Asian American population and
its attempts at cultural self-definition at a historic moment.

Across the Pacific came at an interesting juncture in the history of Asian
American art. Emerging first in the sixties with the rise of Asian
American studies as a discipline, awareness of Asian American art as a
distinct entity has spread and deepened dramatically in the last decade.
Increasingly, many Asian Americans working in the visual arts—artists,
curators, administrators, and critics—have come to function as a com-

1
*Across the Pacific:
Contemporary Korean and
Korean American Art*, orga-
nized by The Queens Museum
of Art, New York; originally on
view October 15, 1993 -
January 9, 1994. *Eds.*

2
*Beyond Boundaries: First
National Asian American Arts
Conference*, organized by
Asian Arts Alliance, New York,
December 17-18, 1993. *Eds.*

3
*Asia/America: Identities in
Asian American Art*, organized
by Asia Society, New York, and
guest curator Margo Machida;
originally on view February 16 -
June 26, 1994. *Eds.*

munity, forging ties with each other through group activities and demar-
cating a critical space for the articulation of an Asian American culture.

Clearly, these developments are intimately linked to the history of Asian
immigration to the U.S. Constituting one of the fastest growing immigrant groups, Asian Americans have reached a critical mass that has
registered its effects not only on the U.S. census but economically,
socially, and politically on the very foundations of U.S. society. Shaped
by its own pattern of immigration and settlement, by the transmittal of
traditions and practices often at variance with mainstream American
culture, and by the burden of discriminatory policies and the onerous
label of being a "model minority," Asian Americans have come to recognize their particular role on the stage of American race relations. Asian
American art has been given impetus by and in turn responded to the
complexities of such issues.

Undoubtedly, the evolution of Asian American art as a phenomenon is
tied also to the rise of identity politics in the U.S. and to the fractious
debates that have developed around the concept of multiculturalism. It is
these developments, which have rocked academia and other cultural
establishments for a decade, that gave rise to last year's Whitney
Biennial [1993], a cultural by-product of American identity politics that
was later, quite surprisingly to some observers, exported to Korea. This
was an exhibition whose attempt to reflect the cultural diversity of
American society was almost universally panned by the mainstream press.

Although many Asian American activists and cultural producers champion
the overall goals of identity politics, opinions can nonetheless be mixed.
Some feel that by raising issues of "difference" if only to challenge
them, identity politics has demarcated more clearly than ever the gap
between the center and the margin on the one hand, and the separate

spheres occupied by various "minorities" of the margin on the other. The desire to establish commonalities and form alliances among members of one racial group is thus offset by misgivings about the tendency toward generalization and self-marginalization. There is, correspondingly, a degree of caution about designating "Asian American art" as such. Given the tremendous diversity of cultures and ethnicities grouped under the rubric, no agreement has been reached as to what constitutes Asian American art—beyond the racial identity of its producers—or how it could be best served.

Within this context, *Across the Pacific* stood out for providing a critical framework that was at once concise and expansive. For one, the exhibition singled out a particular group within the Asian American population, that is, Korean Americans, as the subject of an in-depth examination. At the same time, however, these artists were exhibited alongside their contemporaries from Korea. The combination of these two strategies runs counter to prevailing curatorial practices in the U.S. While there have been some small-scale or historic exhibitions dedicated to specific ethnic groups, the predominant trend has been to address Asian American art as a single and singular field. Energy on both organizational and critical fronts has, for the most part, been dedicated to the definition and promotion of Asian American art as a whole. As a result, Asian American artists have seldom been examined in relation to their peers from Asia. By the same token, exhibitions of contemporary Asian artists have also been exclusively "foreign affairs," rarely making room for what is commonly designated as Asian American art. As suggested by its title, *Across the Pacific* made literal the crossing of such boundaries, adopting a bipartite structure that tentatively broke down the restrictions of an either/or—either Asian or Asian American—discourse. In the process, it suggested provocative ways of rethinking both contemporary Asian and Asian American art.

This was an aspect of *Across the Pacific* which seemed to be missed by *The New York Times*. In a generally positive review, its critic described the exhibition as "a narrowly focused exhibition stressing the same political themes of ethnic and sexual identity that have been ubiquitous among New York artists in the last few years."[4] However subtle, the critic expressed a certain degree of déjà vu with regard to this state of affairs. Although he was accurate in identifying the recurrence of certain pervasive themes in *Across the Pacific*, it would seem that the currents of American identity politics had blinded this critic to the exhibition's novel format, which brought to the fore the correspondences as well as differences between the Korean and Korean American artists. One of these differences, it could be argued, was precisely the absence of a strict discourse of "ethnic" identity in the work of the Korean artists. Divergence on this and other issues raises significant questions for the formulation of a definition of Asian American art and the presumptions on which it has generally been based.

For an observer based in the U.S., perhaps one of the most striking aspects of *Across the Pacific* was the work of the Min Joong artists. Even when transplanted to a foreign context, the fervor and conviction of this revolutionary art are unmistakable. Its bold images and blunt messages provide compelling proof of the instrumental role that art can play in social critique. By detailing the bloodshed and inequities suffered under a repressive regime, works like those by Bong Joon Kim and Jong Gu Lee convey a sense not only of outrage but of the possibility for change. This is an art that speaks to the people and seeks to incite them to action.

4
Holland Cotter, "Korean Works Coming to Terms with the West," *The New York Times*, 10 December 1993, p. 30.

All photos courtesy The Queens Museum of Art, New York

Jong Gu Lee
Farmer is Base of the World II—Chronology, 1984
Acrylic on burlap paper, collage
67 x 39"

It is this voice of solidarity which seems to characterize many of the works by the Korean artists in *Across the Pacific*, a solidarity aimed at wrenching power away from those who misuse it in order to enact it for the common good. Even in works which eschew overt political agendas, there is a distinct sense of this desire and belief in the unitary—in Korea as a land inhabited by a certain populace bound by the same history and destiny. In Hong Joo Kim's *Untitled* of 1992, the face of a lone man blown-up below a scene of rural life speaks to this conception of the people as one entity. Contrary to what the critic for *The New York Times* implied, then, the issue at stake in the work of Korean artists is not ethnic but national identity. The allegiances here are not drawn along racial lines but along national ones, even if debate continues as to who should govern the nation and on whose behalf. Given Korea's recent past, it is clear that this discourse of nationalism is intimately linked to the issue of reunification which has been so important for a divided nation.

Hong Joo Kim
Untitled, 1992
Oil and acrylic on canvas
44 x 57"

The work of the Korean American artists in *Across the Pacific* occupies a markedly different terrain. Instead of outlining the nation as an integrated site, Korean American artists point to a locale that does not have such continuity, whose contours are partial, fragmented, and patchworked. They portray the experiences of those who, in traveling distances from there to here, from Korea to the U.S., still exist in an amorphous zone in-between. They portray also the complexities and tensions of a multi-ethnic society that is simultaneously composed of and splintered by diverse interests and claims. It is in this fashion that ethnic identity comes to the fore. David Chung's wall drawings, for example, explore the heterogeneity intrinsic to such a society. Like cinematic montage, his dynamic compositions fuse a melange of images and vignettes, borrowed from American mass media and urban culture as well as Korean history and family life, to reflect the cacophonous, hybrid quality of Korean American experience. Sung Ho Choi's installation *Choi's Market* addresses such issues more starkly. His burnt-out produce store is a blunt reminder of the 1992 Los Angeles riots/civil unrest, one of the effects of which was to pit African and Korean Americans against each other.

photo: D. James Dee

Sung Ho Choi
Choi's Market, 1993
Wood, photographs, awning, living plants
100 x 150 x 50"

Although Choi addresses a conflict that is—unfortunately—widespread, it seems extremely telling that he inserts an image of his own family in his installation. Like him, many of the Korean American artists in *Across the Pacific* speak in an intensely personal and autobiographical voice. Jin Me Yoon and Young Kim, especially, draw exclusively from their own history to explore the experience of migration. Through family letters and photographic portraits, Yoon captures the anxieties and ambivalence experienced by those who are continually negotiating the gaps of difference. This work resonates beyond solipsistic concerns and reflects the sense of dislocation shared by many, yet its extremely private purview also points to certain boundaries, suggesting the difficulty of simply locating one's own place when confronted daily by multiple allegiances and identities. This approach is in stark contrast to that of the Korean artists. For instead of adopting an expansive, national vision, Korean American artists seek to articulate a sense of selfhood, one that is difficult to define precisely because it is not delimited by a unified national or even ethnic consciousness. Autobiography becomes the primary mode through which the contradictions of such a fractured identity are grappled.

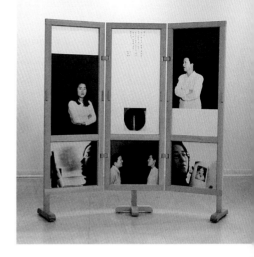

Jin Me Yoon
Screens, 1992 (detail)
Wood, photographic mylar, fabric, cotton, stuffing, framed tests
60 x 60 1/2" each

Yet another way in which the Korean and Korean American artists diverged was in their use and reference to various forms of language. Here, language is conceived in its broadest sense, encompassing not only linguistic communication but also other forms of expression. In this respect, it was striking how vital various traditional "languages" remained for the Korean artists in *Across the Pacific*. Both Ho Suk Kim and Min Hwa Choi, for example, utilize the brushwork and motifs of traditional Korean painting with assurance and fluency. Certainly, many Korean artists also employ aesthetic media and styles—such as oil painting—generally associated with the West. Nonetheless, forms of aesthetic expression derived from a Korean tradition remain available if not for straight adaptation, then at least for quotation and redirection to new uses. This sense of cultural patrimony is, by contrast, conspicuously absent in the work of Korean American artists included in *Across the*

Pacific. Instead they approach language in a much more critical and ironic fashion. Byron Kim, for example, adopts the language of Western abstract painting, while calling into question the universal meanings which have been ascribed to it. Kim reveals how even the format of the monochrome—the most reductive mode of abstraction—can assume culturally specific inflections. Similarly, Michael Joo utilizes a scientific or technical language in order to interrogate its aura of authority and objectivity. Joo's work reveals how the seeming neutrality of such codes can be used precisely to disguise and enforce ethnocentric values. The work of Mo Bahc and Jin Lee explores the role of language in more explicit fashion. Bahc's installation, comprised of video English lessons rife with mistranslations and malapropisms, is a humorous send-up of the challenges of acquiring a new language. In *Book of Names*, Jin Lee lists various terms—Asian, artist, Korean, woman, American—in multiple configurations to show how the designation of identity through language itself shifts and mutates, taking on various nuances in different contexts. Living within a "multilingual" society, these Korean American artists investigate the break-up of language as a coherent system of meaning.

Mo Bahc
Learning American II, 1993
Video projection, flags, electric fans
84 x 132 x 12"

Questions of gender and sexuality also surface in the work of Korean and Korean American artists in ways that are dissimilar, although more subtly so. Both Suk Nam Yun and Soo Kyung Lee provide powerful critiques of a patriarchal society. Yun addresses the issue from the perspective of a traditional Confucian culture which has historically erased women from its social hierarchy, and Lee from the vantage point of a

photo: D. James Dee

Suk Nam Yun
Genealogy, 1993
Acrylic on wood, paper
126 x 110 1/4"

Yong Soon Min
Ritual Labor of a Mechanical Bride, 1993
Mixed media with audio tape
68 x 24 x 24"

modernized society that has enlisted women into the workforce and yet still assigns them to constricting roles. Yong Soon Min's *Ritual Labor of a Mechanical Bride* addresses many similar concerns. However, as a Korean American woman, she also looks beyond gender to suggest how it becomes entangled with issues of race. By using English as the language of entreaty and seduction for her mechanical Korean bride, Yong directs her critique to the Western, male gaze, under which Asian women have been historically constructed as passive, exotic objects of desire.

Although *Across the Pacific* can not be taken as representative of all Korean and Korean American art—the curators stated clearly that their themes were limited to sociopolitical ones and to questions of identity—the exhibition was nonetheless instructive and suggested some ways of thinking critically not only about Korean and Korean American art, but more broadly about Asian and Asian American art. It pointed, above all, to significant differences in the ways in which identity and cultural practice are to be conceived within and outside a national context. What was striking in the work of the Korean artists was its assumption of what might be called a national consciousness, one that is accompanied by and expressed through consolidated cultural traditions. Such a consciousness is far from static or idealized, for it was shown, in many cases, to be located in conflict—between different political powers, between men and women, between Korea itself and the forces of transglobal capitalism. Nonetheless, its outlines continue to hold shape and have resonance even within such debates. In the work of Korean American artists, by contrast, what emerged was not so much a distinctive Korean American identity, but the difficulties and contradictions of articulating a position that is fundamentally unstable and mutable, one that is both and neither Korean or American.

For many, the task of defining both Asian and Asian American art has been an uneasy one, especially in relation to the Western mainstream. Steps toward such definitions are necessary for more in-depth critical dialogues but present many risks, above all the risk of reduplicating restrictive terms that tend toward broad generalizations, thereby reinforcing the relation between center and periphery. The challenge has been to articulate the relationships within the work of Asian and Asian American artists, while at the same time resisting the ossification of categories of identity. *Across the Pacific* showed that avenues exist through which such a process can fruitfully begin.

1994

Disorienting Territories

Race, gender, and sexuality are each distinct sites of struggle in the politics of difference. But it is in the intersection of these domains that some of the most tangled questions of identity reside. Such is the complex territory that Asian women occupy. Confronted by the dominance of both ethnocentric and patriarchal values, theirs is a position that is doubly circumscribed. How, then, do they negotiate and tease apart these overlapping boundaries? How do they speak to the experience of being both Asian and women?

(dis)ORIENTED: Shifting Identities of Asian Women in America, a two-part exhibition presented in New York at the Steinbaum Krauss Gallery and the Henry Street Settlement Abrons Arts Center,[1] explored these questions from a transcultural perspective. Organized by the artist and curator Margo Machida, it brought together fourteen Asian American women artists, along with two male artists who work in collaboration. While some of the artists are recent immigrants, others trace their family ties in Asia two or three generations back. For these women, who inhabit an in-between space straddling disparate cultures and societies, the effects of cultural dislocation have made the ground of identity ever more volatile. Charting this territory at a time when global migrations are rapidly increasing, *(dis)ORIENTED* tackled important and difficult questions about how race, gender, and sexuality are mediated by a transcultural self.

Given that these complicated issues have received scant attention, Machida describes the exhibition as a provisional foray aimed, as she explains in the catalogue, at providing "an open-ended forum that could accommodate diverse expressions." This broadly defined purview

1
Originally on view at Henry Street Settlement Abrons Arts Center and Steinbaum Krauss Gallery, New York, June 24 - July 28, 1995. *Eds.*

notwithstanding, a few recurring themes emerged. A number of artists represented in the exhibition, for example, direct their critique towards the sexual economy, both literal and metaphorical, that underpins Orientalist discourses. Filipina American artist Genara Banzon's sprawling installation, addressing the plight of mail-order brides in her homeland, targets this problem in its most flagrant manifestation. The work is made up of a mock wedding altar surrounded by a motley array of objects and images, including picturesque postcards of the island country and titillating advertisements for bar girls geared to U.S. servicemen stationed there. These are tokens of a Western male imagination, in which visions of a distant tropical paradise intermingled with fantasies of exotic pliant women feed on possessive longings and acquisitive desires.

photo: Adam Reich

Hung Liu
Voyager, 1991
Pastel on paper and wood
42 1/2 x 65 1/2"
Courtesy Steinbaum Krauss Gallery, New York

In a similar vein, Chinese American artist Hung Liu compares the commodification of women to the unequal exchange of power in Sino-Western relations. In *Voyager*, she links a cut-out of Columbus's flagship, the *Santa María*, to two drawings based on turn-of-the-century photographs: one of Chinese prostitutes and the other of foreign troops which stormed into Beijing to quash a local rebellion against imperialist forces. Pointing to the aggressive, expansionary drive that inaugurated an age of European colonialist ventures, the artist constructs a metaphor, as Machida explains, in which "women whose lives were defined by an utter absence of independent action personify the condition of a nation that had virtually lost control of its destiny." But Liu's work also suggests another reading. On a symbolic register, it signifies the mutual reinforcement of racial and gender tropes, whereby the East has historically been feminized and rendered passive in relation to a "virile" West.

Although these works single out Western, male viewpoints and exploits as primary targets of criticism, most of the artists in the exhibition look beyond a divisive East-versus-West paradigm. That the photographs of Chinese prostitutes used in Hung Liu's work were produced originally for the consumption of their own countrymen suggests the complex interplay of sexist attitudes across racial divides. Thus, women's marginal position in Asian cultures also comes under equal scrutiny and attack. In *Lesbian Precepts*, for example, Vietnamese American artist Hanh Thi Pham contests restrictive aspects of the Asian cultural legacy by subverting its male-centered symbolic systems. In a revolt against Asian (as well as Western) religious traditions "where God has to be a man," the artist presents herself as Buddha, with her legs folded in a lotus position and her hands held in iconic gestures. Around this personal altar, Pham displays a magnified microscopic image of her vaginal fluid and a monthly menstruation chart. These components of Pham's work are intended as bold affirmations of her sexuality as a woman and as a lesbian. They are

photo: Daniel Mirer

Hanh Thi Pham
Lesbian Precepts, 1995
Mixed media
97 1/2 x 85 x 12"

troubling, however, in that they play into deterministic stereotypes about women's biological make-up.

The collaborative work of Monica Chau and Daniel Mirer seeks to sidestep such reductive codings by adopting a more self-reflexive stance. Chau, a second-generation Chinese American, and Mirer, a third-generation Jewish American, employ their own experience as a real-life couple as inspiration for their work. In *Lofan/Shikseh*, a piece which combines text with photographic self-portraits, they recount the discomfort and irritation expressed by both their parents when informed of the budding interracial romance between the pair. These anecdotes are printed on curtains which may be drawn open or closed—a presentation device which evokes the veiling and unveiling of hidden prejudices. No matter how subtle, the artists suggest, it is these mutual misconceptions harbored by and against all groups which reinforce the barriers of racial and sexual difference.

For a number of artists in the exhibition, this integration of subject matter and formal structure appears to be something of a stumbling block. The works in *(dis)ORIENTED* are rich in references, as was the exhibition as a whole. They grapple with the dense histories and intricate issues that shape Asian American women's lives. But sometimes, as in Genara Banzon's installation, an artist attempts to jam-pack so much into a work that it loses coherence and impact. Sometimes, as in Hung Liu's work, images are simply cobbled together. Though informative, the approach is as bland as textbook illustrations. In attempting to provide a thorough overview of its rarely explored topic, *(dis)ORIENTED* yielded many stimulating insights but also revealed the difficulty of balancing pedagogy with resonant artistic practices.

Mimi Young
Untitled (flip-side), 1995
C-print
26 1/2 x 40"

By far the most successful works in the exhibition were the ones which synthesized message and medium to push each in unpredictable and illuminating ways. On this score, the work of Chinese American artist Mimi Young is especially memorable. The subject of her photographic series is a curious knick-knack—a chopstick rest in the form of a supine child of ambiguous gender. (Young describes the figure as a woman, though there are no apparent features that would distinguish it as such. How viewers decode the object in gender terms becomes a fascinating aspect of the work itself.) These elegant yet enigmatic images invoke the fetishistic attachments entwined in objectifying views of the Other. Yet by photographing the ceramic ware from a variety of angles to juxtapose its glossy surface against its crude underside, Young calls these feelings into tantalizing play only to expose and disrupt them.

Lynne Yamamoto
Absent, 1992-1995
Artificial hair, cast glass, clay pots,
soil, grass, photograph
Dimensions variable

Another highlight of the exhibition was the work of Japanese American artist Lynne Yamamoto. Her installation *Absent* is composed of three elements: a jumbled mass of black hair which falls from ceiling to floor; seven clay plots with live grass from which glass castings of

77

the artist's ear protrude; and a tiny drawing of a woman in kimono with her hands held over her mouth. As Machida explains, the work is informed by the life and hardships of Yamamoto's grandmother, who arrived in Hawaii as a picture bride. Even without this explicit gloss, *Absent* conveys lyrically the sense of hope and renewal that persists in face of the tangled predicaments and repressive silence to which Asian women have been subjected. Despite uneven patches, *(dis)ORIENTED* was a pioneering exhibition which deserves recognition for breaking this silence.

1996

The Plurality of Contemporary Asian Art

Amid great fanfare, the Asia Society unveiled its mega exhibition of contemporary Asian art *Contemporary Art in Asia: Traditions/Tensions* in New York in October 1996. The local press anointed the exhibition even before it officially opened. Most notably, *The New York Times* devoted one of its most coveted spots—the front page of its cultural section—to advance coverage of the show. As the headline trumpeted, this was "The Brave New Face of Art From the East." The hubbub was a measure of the heightened expectations attached to the show.

Indeed, *Traditions/Tensions* presented a new and unfamiliar face to most audiences in New York. Despite the apparent vogue for multiculturalism and the fashionable embrace of global trends, until recently American art establishments have shown relatively little interest in contemporary art from Asia. When they have, the focus has usually been restricted to the art of individual Asian countries.

The Asia Society set a bigger goal for itself. Adopting a broad multinational perspective, it brought together a diverse range of contemporary artworks from across the Asian region. The statistics of the exhibition alone—twenty-seven artists and fifty-nine works in a variety of media—indicate the ambitious scope of the Asia Society's undertaking. At such a scale, the exhibition necessitated collaboration with two other institutions in the city, New York University's Grey Art Gallery and the Queens Museum of Art. The exhibition was presented simultaneously at all three venues.[1]

How, then, does one make sense of this vast territory? Especially a territory that has received so little exposure in the United States?

1
Originally on view simultaneously at Asia Society, October 4, 1996 - February 2, 1997; Grey Art Gallery and Study Center, New York University, October 4 - December 21, 1996; and The Queens Museum of Art, October 4, 1996 - February 16, 1997. *Eds.*

Organized under the direction of the Thai critic and art historian, Apinan Poshyananda, *Traditions/Tensions* took shape through a number of curatorial decisions and strategies. The results were somewhat mixed. In both its strengths and its shortcomings, *Traditions/Tensions* revealed the challenges of representing the art of an entire region, even selectively, to foreign audiences. It highlighted the difficulties, on both logistical and conceptual fronts, of organizing twenty-seven Asian artists within a coherent exhibition framework.

One key decision taken by the Asia Society was to limit the exhibition to five countries in Asia: India, Indonesia, the Philippines, South Korea and Thailand. The selection seemed peculiar, at least on paper. This geographic spread was neither comprehensive, nor did it observe the usual geo-political divisions within the region. Thus, the exhibition teamed one country each from East Asia and South Asia with three countries from Southeast Asia, areas which would seem to have followed quite disparate paths in terms of culture, politics, history and religion.

The exhibition literature offered a specific rationale for this orientation. As it stated, *Traditions/Tensions* was not intended to provide "a homogeneous survey of regional trends." Instead, it selected five countries to "suggest not only the diversity of this vast area but also the surprising similarity of intent demonstrated by some artists from quite different contexts." Thus, the exhibition grouped artists together on the basis of shared issues and approaches, rather than national affiliation. Within this context, *Traditions/Tensions* focused on three recurrent themes—religious forms and ideas; gender issues; and colonial history and contemporary realities. Moreover, at least according to the introductory wall texts at each exhibition site, these themes were divided among the three venues in distinct groupings. In reality, however, these divisions were far from neat.

Whether by design or by default—due perhaps to space limitations and other practical constraints that large-scale exhibitions often confront—the artworks presented did not always conform to the designated thematic category of each site. This deviation seemed particularly acute at the Queens Museum of Art and the Grey Art Gallery. Although a looser, more associative approach can yield a richer reading of artworks in certain contexts, such a possibility was hampered by the exhibition's division among three distant exhibition sites. As a result, the surrender of thematic logic in *Traditions/Tensions* exacerbated the sense of dissonance and confusion in some parts of the exhibition.

The Queens Museum of Art, for example, was supposed to present pieces that address "the intermixing of ethnic, racial, and religious groups as well as issues of gender," according to the introductory wall text. In actuality, the works in this sprawling presentation reflected a much wider and more complex array of issues. FX Harsono's photographic installation *Voice With a Voice/Sign*, for example, is directed against the political repression in Indonesia, which it protests by spelling out the hope for democracy. Korean artist Choi Jeong-hwa's *The Death of a Robot*, by contrast, mocks the myth of Asia's industrial prowess and economic prosperity through the form of a giant balloon robot,

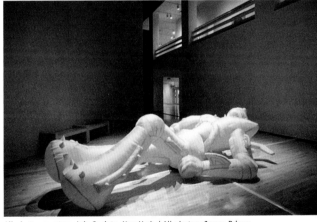

All photos courtesy Asia Society, New York / All photos: James Prince

Choi Jeong-Hwa
"About Being Irritated"—The Death of a Robot, 1995
Fabric, air compressor, oil-pressure equipment, movement timer, CD player with speakers
275 5/8 x 78 3/4 x 196 7/8"

81

Chatchai Puipia
Mae Chow Woil, 1994
Oil on canvas
59 x 43 1/4"

which is inflated only to be deflated again and again. The grimaces of the crouching man in Thai artist Chatchai Puipia's paintings register, on an individual psychic level, the rage, isolation and anxiety experienced in a society of rapid change and flux. Kim Ho-suk's ethereal paintings, on the other hand, adopt a collective view and commemorate episodes from Korea's recent history as a tenacious memory.

Of course, a one-line description in a wall text cannot encompass the richness of the best works of art. It can only function as an aid in pedagogy and a shorthand for interpretation. And the works of Choi, Kim and Harsono are, each in its own right, powerful and thought-provoking. Yet the works at the Queens Museum reflected such disparate approaches and vantage points that the exhibition as a whole often seemed scattered and disjointed. A bit of global economics and Korean history here, and a bit of Indonesian politics and Indian religion there. That each work incorporated intricate social and cultural references yielded fascinating new insights, but also made the exhibition difficult to digest and synthesize. Without a clearly delineated curatorial perspective, the exhibition failed to provide the fullest opportunity for deeper understanding.

Into the mix at the Queens Museum, the organizers also placed a number of works that related to issues of gender. In the installation by the Korean artist Kim Soo-ja, for example, the scattered bundles of brightly colored cloth embody the practice and role of women's work. The accompanying videos which show the artist moving silently through

Kim Soo-Ja
Sewing into Walking, 1994
Used clothing, bed cover, TV monitor, closed-circuit camera,
video projector, CD player
473 x 394"

repetitive tasks—walking, circling a courtyard, and gathering pieces of
cloth along a riverbank—extend her metaphors into a broader rumination on life's rhythm and flow. Sheela Gowda's work utilizes a
very different type of material—cow dung—to suggest the rituals
and domestic chores practiced by women in India, and to evoke the
sacred traditions and the potential for healing inscribed in the
space of the everyday. Both of these artists adopt a meditative
tone, which resonates through their subtle visual poetics. Their jux-
taposition with the more visually aggressive works at the Queens
Museum, however, often seemed jarring.

This type of visual disharmony had the opposite effect from what the
organizers intended. Aware that the specific cultural references in each
work might not be apparent to first-time visitors, as the exhibition
brochure explained, the organizers hoped the works' "visual language
[would] be potent enough to transcend national and cultural boundaries." The exhibition's often awkward installations and juxtapositions,
however, undermined this potential at a number of turns.

Kamol Phaosavasdi
Mode of Moral Being, 1995-1996
7 mosquito nets, 1 wooden trolley, video player, 4 monitors, 5 tape
players, headphones, lights, plaster, stone, wood box, photograph, photocopy
100 x 200 x 240"

N. N. Rimzon
The Inner Voice, 1992
Resin, fiberglass, marble dust, cast iron
Dimensions variable

The problem was also evident at the Grey Art Gallery. On the first level of the exhibition space, paintings by Nalini Malani, I Wayan Bendi and Bhupen Khakhar formed a less than successful mix. Their placement made the paintings' muddy colors into a failing rather than an attribute. Some works in the exhibition, such as Kamol Phaosavasdi's installation which addressed the problem of prostitution in Thailand, simply functioned better as a didactic vehicle than as a visual statement.

Of the three parts of *Traditions/Tensions* the Asia Society presentation was the most unified thematically and visually. Here, the works addressed the role of religion and utilized religious forms variously as a means of spiritual reflection, social commentary and political critique. Ravinder Reddy's statues adopt the forms of Indian temple sculpture in the service of a

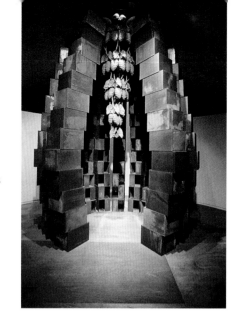

Montien Boonma
Alokhayasan: Temple of Mind, 1995-1996
Installation with metal lungs, herbs, pigments, glue
128 x 106 x 106"

new kind of portraiture. The bright color, stark expression and ambiguous posture of his figures—all of them women in this exhibition—do not offer any religious calm. Instead, their disquieting presence suggests the experiences of contemporary dislocation. N. N. Rimzon's *The Inner Voice* is composed simply of a stone statue surrounded by a ring of swords. A commentary on recent religious riots in India, the work's abbreviated vocabulary and unexpected restraint starkly convey the threat of violence and conflict. In *Alokhayasan: Temple of Mind*, Montien Boonma created a serene sanctuary infused with the healing smell of herbs. The ephemerality and simplicity of Boonma's means emanate a generosity of spirit which proves the adage that "less is more." These and other works at the Asia Society reveal the complex role of religious tradition in contemporary Asia, where inherited beliefs can sustain as well as clash with contemporary values.

In the end, perhaps, the most invaluable thing that *Traditions/Tensions* provided was the opportunity to see contemporary works from Asia at first hand. Considering the logistics involved, this was no small feat. And the exhibition brought some remarkable works to New York, from Choi Jeong-hwa's acerbically kitsch extravaganzas and Reamillo & Juliet's biting critiques of the conflict of power, on sexual and political fronts, to Cho Duck Hyun's haunting installation about the possibility of historical remembrance and renewal, among many others. *Traditions/Tensions* also illuminated facets of contemporary Asian art and culture that might have been otherwise obscured in an exhibition which observed conventional tropes and geo-political divisions. If the exhibition had paired Korean artists with their East Asian contemporaries, for example, the legacy of colonialization in Asia would have taken on a different valence.

In his essay for the exhibition's catalogue, Apinan begins with a description of the multifarious facets of contemporary Asia. "There are so many sides to Asia," he states, "that it can be at times elusive, confusing and contradictory." Apinan created an exhibition which preserves this sense of complexity. ("The Brave New Face of Art from the East" is not singular but plural.) Whatever its flaws, *Traditions/Tensions* resisted simplistic generalities, highlighting the tensions and dynamic forces that propel contemporary Asian art and culture. In so doing, it compelled us to think about the art, long after the exhibition.

1997

Critical Essays

Godzilla: The Anarchistic Lizard

In the three years since its inception, the arts group Godzilla has become an ubiquitous presence in the Asian American art community. Its meetings are frequently packed, and its newsletter distributed to scores of people. Although primarily based in New York, Godzilla has also drawn attention nationally and internationally, with inquiries coming from as far as London and Tokyo.

Known formally as Godzilla: Asian American Art Network, the group performs a wide range of roles. It is equally a clearing house for information and exhibition opportunities, an organ through which different opinions within a diverse community are aired and examined, and an advocacy group which promotes the work of Asian American artists to a wider public. It is also known to throw a good party or two.

Godzilla is, foremost among its many functions, a forum that fosters communication and support among Asian American artists. Towards that end, it hosts regular meetings and slide talks where artists present and discuss their work. "Many people live in isolated pockets," artist Lynne Yamamoto states, expressing a common sentiment in the New York art world, which can be daunting in its enormity and indifference. "It's reassuring to know there's a supportive group of artists who are Asian." It is also important, as another artist, Carol Sun, points out, to test out and "analyze ideas with a group who shares similar concerns."

Beyond acting as a support system, Godzilla has also sought to stimulate debates on broader issues of critical and theoretical interest, primarily through the format of panel discussions. One panel, for example, posed the notion of an "Asian American aesthetic" as a concept that might be identified and isolated apart from other aesthetic styles. In lively and sometimes controversial discussions such as this, Godzilla panels have raised some of the most thorny questions about the impact of race on art.

Godzilla has extended this exchange of ideas to the written word as well, by publishing a newsletter which includes reviews and comprehensive listings of exhibitions alongside more in-depth articles. The newsletter addresses the basic lack of documentation and scholarship which has inhibited the development of the field of Asian American art as such.

Inasmuch as Godzilla's activities are aimed mainly at its members, the group is also highly aware of its role as a liaison to institutions and individuals outside the community. As Ken Chu, an artist and co-founder of Godzilla, argues, "the mainstream doesn't perceive us as contemporary artists. It pigeonholes us as traditional artists." Godzilla has helped to heighten the visibility of contemporary Asian American artists, by maintaining a slide registry and serving as a central resource for curators, granting agencies, and other organizations. In the process it has become something of a "spokesperson" for the Asian American art community.

The name which the group chose for itself indicates the activist stance of its founders. A monster that threatens to topple everything in its way, Godzilla is a creature out to get what it wants, counter to the stereotype of passivity associated with Asian people. The name Godzilla, made popular through B-movies of the sixties, also captures the ironic humor and high spirits of the group.

Godzilla's formation in 1990 emerged from discussions among an informal group of artists, curators, and writers, who stated in the inaugural issue of the newsletter: "We must develop forums capable of addressing our needs as artists." Implicit in this statement is the recognition that such needs have not been met by mainstream institutions in the U.S.

The exclusivity of mainstream institutions, and of Western canons in general, has stirred intense cultural debates in the U.S. in the last few years. In a scathing critique published in *Arts Magazine* in 1990, for example, long-time art critic John Yau cited the all-white roster of the 1991 Whitney Biennial and declared that the museum "has decided to remain an institution that ignores cultural difference." The restriction of the cultural landscape to a predominantly white, male perspective, blind to the demographic heterogeneity of American society, has provoked an examination of the power structure of American cultural politics. At the same time, the situation has prompted not only Asian American but also Latino, African, and Native American artists to focus on their racial identity as an issue to be explored in art.

In part, it is this cultural context which gave rise to a group like Godzilla. One of the first steps Godzilla took was a letter it wrote in 1991 to David Ross, the newly-appointed director of the Whitney Museum of American Art. "To be truly reflective of the major demographic and cultural shifts in our society is to recognize the rapidly expanding population of Asians and Asian Americans whose artistic vitality is reshaping American culture," Godzilla wrote. "The failure of the 1991 Biennial to acknowledge our contributions makes its claims to diversity and inclusivity ring hollow."

Two years later, art historian Eugenie Tsai looks back on that strategy of protest. Tsai believes that the letter "had an effect." It "made [Ross] extremely aware of us" and "hit an administration which was receptive and willing to entertain these complaints." Significantly, the 1993 Whitney Biennial included a much more racially diverse list of artists. Although it also elicited some of the most severe criticisms in the exhibition's history, indicating a degree of resistance on the part of the mainstream.

Other factors have also contributed to the formation of Godzilla. As Margo Machida, an artist, curator, and co-founder of Godzilla, argues, unlike other racial communities, Asian Americans "still don't have national institutions." Whereas the African American art community can look to the leadership of the Studio Museum in Harlem and the Latino community to El Museo del Barrio, both in New York, Asian American artists have been represented in a more circumscribed fashion by local groups or ethnic-specific organizations. In the absence of a major institution, there is an "urgency for people to create their own frameworks for interpretation."

In the attempt to bring Asian Americans together as a consolidated group with a unique voice of its own, however, Godzilla members are also deeply aware of the diversity of a community shaped by ongoing patterns of immigration. Thus, the organization encompasses first-generation immigrants along with American-born artists. Its geographic scope is also decidedly Pan-Asian, extending from East Asia to South and Southeast Asia. (The preferred nomenclature for some is the more inclusive term "Asian Pacific Islander.")

Godzilla members regard this diversity as intrinsic to the character of the group. It is important, Machida remarks, for the group not to be restricted to "a singular idea of community" or to be vested in any one agenda. *The Curio Shop*, for example, an exhibition which Godzilla organized earlier this year at an alternative space in New York, provided a broad framework for the art of forty-eight members, working in vastly different styles. As writer Kerri Sakamoto wrote in the introduction to the catalogue, the exhibition attempted to question the distorted and static forms of representation assigned to Asian Americans. "While the dominant white culture is permitted to be dynamic and to progress," she writes, "other cultures are bound to representations as quaint, primitive, or exotic entities."

In the spirit of diversity and dynamic evolution, Godzilla has remained a loosely structured group. Guided by a steering committee of ten people, it has resisted becoming a formal organization with set hierarchies. Instead, in response to the changing demographics and needs of the Asian American art community, it has embraced the notion of free form and change. As Machida proposes humorously, Godzilla is an "anarchistic lizard." In the broader sense of the word, Godzilla is also an anarchistic force that attempts to break through the isolation and boundaries within which many Asian American artists have had to work.

1994

Asian American Exhibitions Reconsidered

1
Originally presented as a
paper for the panel
"Imag(in)ing Ethnicity: Its
Impact on Cultural Discourse
and Production," Asian Arts
Alliance, New York, December
18, 1993. See *Credits* for
details. *Eds.*

2
*Godzilla: Asian American Art
Network* 3, no. 2 (fall 1993).

A few months ago I was sent a questionnaire by Godzilla, the Asian American Art Network, and asked to evaluate the "viability" of group exhibitions dedicated solely to the work of Asian American contemporary artists.[1] The answers, to be gathered from numerous artists, writers, and curators, were to be published in a special issue of the Godzilla newsletter.[2] That this question itself was posed indicates the high degree of ambivalence that exists in the Asian American art community towards the model of the group exhibition. The answers that Godzilla received, along with mine, were clear about those ambivalences. The statement submitted by the artist Mo Bahc was perhaps emblematic. He wrote simply: "Asian American artists' exhibitions are the kind of shows that I am usually invited to be in. That is the biggest reason that I am in those exhibitions, not that I try hard to be in those shows. That is not to say that there are other kinds of shows I want to be in, or that I am sick of another Asian American or Korean American show. I keep making art. And it is better to show than not to show."

While Bahc indicated an attitude of some tolerance for these exhibitions, his last sentence "it is better to show than not to show" is telling. Group exhibitions that showcase artists from the same racial group have become, for not only Asian Americans but many artists of color, the main venue for their work's exposure. Indeed, these exhibitions can help to increase an artist's visibility and are laudable in this respect. Yet, in the end, they perform a circumscribed role, often serving an institution's interest in balanced programming more than the artist's need for in-depth, critical evaluation. While such exhibitions can be instructive, they are also panaceas for a broader problem—the failure to integrate Asian American artists more fully into a wide range of exhibition formats and other cultural discourses that cut across racial boundaries. They reveal a tendency toward rigid classification along racial lines that can contribute to an ossification of concepts of identity.

In contrast, one might look at a number of recent exhibitions that sought explicitly to interrogate notions of race. Examples of such an approach would include exhibitions such as *Yellow Peril: Reconsidered*, which toured throughout Canada in 1990 and 1991, and *The Curio Shop*, which was organized by Godzilla and presented at Artists Space in New York in the spring of 1993. *Yellow Peril: Reconsidered* featured experimental and documentary photo, film, and video work by Asian Canadians. Clearly, as indicated by its title, this exhibition was intended to rebuke and challenge such stereotypes and labels as the "yellow peril." Thus, its main organizer, Paul Wong, was careful to elucidate the diversity of experiences and cultures that are lumped together under the rubric "Asian Canadian." He writes of the gap, for example, that exists between those born in Canada and recent immigrants to the country. Yet, on the first page of his essay, Wong also writes about "the inferiority complex that has helped shape behavioural practice within our communities." Ultimately, passages such as this betray the limitations of the exhibition's framework. For what has registered with me is not the art in the exhibition but the term "Yellow Peril." The use of such a terminology only perpetuates the attitudes sanctioned by it—an attitude of self-censure that is transformed by Wong into the concept of an "inferiority complex" within his community.

The problems of such an approach may be characterized as one of reductive logic. They are tied, I think, in large measure to the way in which identity politics has developed in both the U.S. and Canada. Evolving alongside this politics, group exhibitions such as *Yellow Peril: Reconsidered* have responded to its preoccupations. In the process, they

The Curio Shop exhibition, 1993
Installation view, Artists Space, New York

have emphasized the social context in which identity is situated and the politically inflected processes of misrepresentation and exclusion. Such exhibitions have, as a result, leaned towards strategies that directly critique mainstream constructions of identity. It is on this level that one is asked to "reconsider" the Yellow Peril. Likewise, *The Curio Shop* at Artists Space aimed at deconstructing the "Oriental curio." While this oppositional approach forms a major part of the postmodernist enterprise, it also treads dangerous waters. For identity is defined here as a form of negation, in opposition to notions of the "norm" or the "stereotype." In the end, reduced to the logic of a closed circuit, this approach grants such tropes a kind of elaboration that only affirms their centrality.

Because art is viewed in this context as a kind of corrective to misrepresentation, the development of identity politics in the cultural arena has also tended to institutionalize particular styles of artmaking. What is often mandated is a style that can easily be read as encoded by race, one that I would characterize as primarily descriptive or illustrative. It is a style that declares its documentary truth value, in many cases, by resorting to figurative imagery, quotations from the media, and textual documentation. In a sense, this is a style that is presumed to be a more "authentic" form of identity. But authentic in what sense? Authentic insofar as it is a narrow response to gaps within dominant representation. Here, I would like to quote another artist, Simon Leung, who wrote to Godzilla: "What strikes me is the demand such a voice of identity places on the viewer (me) during such instances when it is the organizing principle of an exhibition—it announces itself as an authoritative difference. . . . [And] difference, dressed in the armor of authority, is set up to oppose . . . but another difference." Exhibitions such as *Yellow Peril: Reconsidered* only reinscribe difference in the effort to circumvent it.

The question remains: Can the link between race and artistic practice be conceived beyond the logic of simple negation or illustration? Can group exhibitions assist in enunciating forms of identity that are, in other words, not subjugated to the demands of dominant representation? In whatever form, exhibitions are mechanisms for the production of social meaning. Those dedicated to artists of color, in particular, perform a special operation—a kind of ethnographic work in which the contemporary artist becomes an artifact of difference. Perhaps one approach to the problem, then, would be to undo the ethnographic tendency of this format, that is, to shift the emphasis away from race as matter of mere content towards positions of greater complexity and specificity that encompass race as only one of the many components that both shape artistic practice and are addressed by it. A group exhibition that posits race as its only organizing principle always risks essentialism, first of all in its suppression of issues such as nationality, sexuality, religion, and class that make up the complex terrain of identity. More importantly, exhibitions that focus exclusively on race obscure the divergent and contradictory ways in which race itself and its attendant politics are positioned relative to other concerns and strategies. These might include, for example, such questions as how different symbolic structures, ritual practices, and even conceptions of modernist and postmodernist languages have informed the production of visual culture in different communities and by different artists. The task at hand is not to hegemonize the category of race but to decenter it.

1993

Siting China: On Migration and Displacement in Contemporary Art

The theme of migration and displacement has gained increasing currency within academic circles in the last few years. For this century has witnessed, as James Clifford describes it, "a dramatic expansion of mobility."[1] Propelled by multiple forces, populations, goods, and cultures are moving across and reconfiguring the spaces once demarcated by strict national and cultural boundaries. If the term "migration" is descriptive of a particular mode of travel, suggesting the search for a new, permanent domicile, then "displacement" connotes the disruption and disorientation that accompanies such a movement. It suggests the contestation as well as the commingling of disparate values, identities, and practices.[2]

I would like to consider a particular feature within this landscape. The topic—the case study, if you will—is the displacement of China into the West and vice versa. This may seem to be a rather narrow focus, but the case of China is complex for many reasons, beginning, first, with the question of national boundaries. Of course China does designate a particular territory with its structures of national governance. Yet, one must also remember Hong Kong, which has been under British colonial rule but will revert to China in just three years—a change certain to provoke extreme anxieties. Or Taiwan, which has made its claims on China, politically and culturally, although there is also a burgeoning movement to forge a local identity. Because of the complexity of such factors as national boundary, the term China itself thus bears some scrutiny.

It is for this reason that I have chosen the word "China" rather than "Chinese" in the title. "China" is invoked as something, I hope, poten-

1
For writings by James Clifford on this theme, see *Routes: Travel and Translation in the Late Twentieth Century* (Cambridge, Mass.: Harvard University Press, 1997). *Eds.*

2
Originally presented as the introduction to the author's panel of the same name, College Art Association conference, 1994. See *Credits* for details. *Eds.*

tially more flexible and open to play. China becomes here a site of multiple meanings and slippages—considered as a modern nation, an area of consolidated aesthetic and philosophical traditions, a locale marked by particular gender relations, a place of family origin and nostalgic identification, a site within the Western imagination. (The list goes on.) China is a site of cultural, aesthetic, political, economic as well as symbolic dimensions, which overlap as well as contradict each other. The question, then, is as follows: In what ways is China, in all these different senses, constituted in the work of artists in migration from China to the West?[3] Which of these Chinas comes to the fore in their work and in what dimension? How is China sited? Inversely and implicitly, I would also ask: How is the West, in similarly complex definitions of the word, sited?

The question of siting China has many methodological implications as well. It leads to the larger challenge: How do we site China in relation to both global and local frameworks? Clearly, China's situation is not unique. It is subject to many of the same forces that affect other instances of displacement, forces that are centripetal and diffusionary, yet still governed by unequal relations of power and the irregular flow of economic and other resources. Yet, how do we site China within the space and discourse of postmodern, global displacement with its very useful metaphors of hybridity and syncretism, without giving in to the homogenization and generalizations implied by such a move? On the other hand, how do we site China in relation to its local conditions, its specific historical and material features including particular aesthetic traditions, without reinscribing notions of difference, purity, or essence? The awareness of China as a site that is constructed allows us to look more vigilantly at the assumptions underlying both global and local frameworks.

3
Among the artists whose work was discussed at the conference panel for which these remarks were originally written, were Tseng Yu-ho (Betty Ecke), Wu Sanzhuan, Xu Bing, and Gu Wenda. Two other artists, Simon Leung and Zhang Baoji, discussed their own work.

Similar sets of questions can be posed with regard to the siting of China as a field or discipline. As a curator and writer, I have been involved in projects dedicated to the promotion and definition of an Asian-American art. While I support such activities, first of all as a political strategy for gaining visibility for artists, I am also wary of hyphenated terms such as Asian-American or Chinese-American. It seems to me that such terminology can become hardened, designating a fixed quantity that subsumes equal parts of the Asian and of the American. Such terminology gives rise to the popular notion that there can be a simple "synthesis of East and West." Such terminology begs the question of when an immigrant artist turns from being Chinese into being Chinese-American. Such terminology also does not take into account the parallels and relationships that exist between migrant artists in the U.S. and those who are elsewhere, such as Europe.

Perhaps the notion of what is an Asian-American or Chinese-American art would be more fruitfully explored if it were formulated, again, in the following way. How is Asia or China sited in art created by those in migration? How are we to site Chinese artists as well as first, second, and third-generation immigrants in relation to China and in relation to each other?

Similarly, the question of siting China might free us from the constraints of both the fields of traditional Chinese art history and modern Western art criticism, both of which make their claims on Chinese contemporary art, bringing to the enterprise different biases and blinders. We must continually ask how we are to site China in relation to these disciplines. Finally, I would like to suggest that siting China, as indicated by the present progressive tense I employ, is an ongoing and fluid process. I would propose that where and how we site China depends on the changing circumstances, purposes, and subjects of our work. The process of remapping a new geography of mobile contours requires an agile and dexterous hand.

1994

Why Asia?

The possibility of a truly global culture is a question that has occupied critics and theorists for almost a decade now, continuing to provoke contention and debate. If we take the particular case of Asian American art, its development presents an instructive example of the tensions and challenges that arise in the negotiation of disparate cultures, whether within a specifically American context or within a global one.[1]

Awareness of Asian American art as a distinct entity has spread and deepened dramatically in the last decade. The flurry of events which took place in New York during the past year is indicative. There was a national conference as well as two major exhibitions devoted to Asian American art in New York, including *Asia/America*, which is on view at Asia Society across town.[2] Indeed, many Asian Americans working in the field of visual arts—artists, curators, administrators, and critics—have come to function more and more as a community, attempting to forge ties and to demarcate a critical space for the articulation of an Asian American culture.

The emergence of the field is closely linked to the history of Asian immigration to the U.S. Asians now constitute one of the fastest growing immigrant groups in the U.S., reaching a critical mass that has registered its effects not only on the U.S. census but economically, socially, and politically on the very foundations of U.S. society. It is a group shaped by particular experiences—by its own pattern of immigra-tion and settlement, which is quite different when compared, say to that of African Americans; by the transmission of specific cultural traditions and practices often at variance with mainstream American culture; by the burden of being identified as outsiders and a "model minority,"

1
Originally presented as a paper for a panel of the same name, Taipei Gallery, New York, April 15, 1994. See *Credits* for details. *Eds.*

2
Beyond Boundaries: First National Asian American Arts Conference, organized by Asian Arts Alliance, New York, December 17-18, 1993. See "Asian American Exhibitions Reconsidered." *Across the Pacific: Contemporary Korean and Korean American Art*, organized by The Queens Museum of Art, New York; originally on view October 15, 1993 - January 9, 1994. See "Looking for the Identity of Korean Art." *Asia/America: Identities in Asian American Art*, organized by Asia Society, New York, and guest curator Margo Machida; originally on view February 16 - June 26, 1994. *Eds.*

often a cause of friction with other ethnic groups. And so, Asian Americans have come to recognize their unique role on the stage of American race relations. Asian American art has been given impetus by these developments, reflecting its attempts at cultural self-definition at a historic moment.

Yet, within the community itself, opinions have been extremely mixed about the strategies for and efficacy of promoting Asian American art. There is, first of all, little agreement as to what constitutes Asian American art as such. Is it simply a descriptive label referring purely to the racial background of the artist? Or does the term serve a critical purpose designating a kind of art with shared concerns, vocabularies, and histories that imply the combination of Asian and Western modes? If so, what does Asian American art look like? Can there actually be a common denominator, given the many different ethnic groups that are covered under the rubric, not to mention the wide array of interests and stylistic approaches adopted by individual artists? While the term "Asian American" continues to be circulated and adopted, its meanings remain inexact and elusive.

It is not surprising, then, that little consensus exists either as to how Asian American art should be best served. Do group exhibitions devoted exclusively to it help or hinder its cause? Do such exhibitions only demarcate and thus enforce the gap between mainstream and margin? Or do they help to expose questions of difference, and bring visibility to the problems of assimilating into American society? After all, this is a democratic country, but you must speak in order to be heard.

But while the Asian American community debates these issues, treading delicately between the need for alliance and dialogue and the resistance to cliché and self-ghettoization, many critics in the mainstream and popular press continue to misunderstand, ignore, or stereotype its efforts. Take the example of a recent review by Kay Larson which appeared in *New York* magazine, written as a response to the *Asia/America* exhibition.[3] At one point, she states: "The migrants tell of loneliness, sleeping on floors, working at dull jobs, learning that nobody cares. Sounds familiar, doesn't it? I could sympathize, and I do, but what did they expect?" I have my own reservations about the exhibition, but there is a sense of latent hostility in Larson's review. "Go home if you don't like this country," she seems to imply.

My point is not so much that critics are biased, but that the wider dissemination of art by Asian Americans in this country is still fraught with contradictions and difficulties. At the same time that Asian American artists try to articulate their own position within this society, they run the risk of reducing it into a formulaic set of generalities. Trying to open up a space for critical discussion within their own community, they run the risk of isolation and segregation. But if they do not do all of this, then they also lose the possibility of articulating the distinctiveness of their experience and culture, and they run the risk of invisibility and incomprehension. Whatever they do, their position in relation to the mainstream remains highly ambivalent.

This situation has many parallels to the question of a global culture. Recently I organized a panel for the College Art Association on Chinese artists who have immigrated to the West.[4] I was struck by their evolution. While in China, they produced works that engaged directly with Chinese philosophy and social conditions. In the West, they shifted their approach and vocabularies to modes that are much more readily identified as Western. The change was motivated by the desire to respond to new audiences in the West. But in the process, much of the challenge and power of their work was also lost. They revealed to me

3
Kay Larson, "Asia Minor," *New York* 27, no. 10 (March 7, 1994), p. 80.

4
See "Siting China." *Eds.*

105

how difficult it is for Asian art to enter into a dialogue with the West without losing a sense of its cultural and historical specificity. Yet, how could it not respond to the complexities of its present moment, of its evolving relationship to the West, without reproducing a vision that is static or nostalgic? Western norms continue to monopolize many critical discussions, posing as the standard by which most art is judged and admitted into circulation. If there is going to be a truly global culture, then we are still some time away from it.

1994

Beyond Nation and Tradition:
Art in Post-Mao China

When Asia Society invited me to participate in a symposium on the occasion of its exhibition, *Contemporary Art in Asia: Traditions/Tensions*, I have to confess that I found myself in a bit of a dilemma.[1] The dilemma had to do with the dual nature of my task. On the one hand, I was asked to address the question of "Modernism and the Reinvention of 'Tradition'" which was the topic of my assigned panel. On the other, I was invited specifically to talk about contemporary art in China, particularly in the realm of non-official art, with which I am most familiar. From my point of view, however, these two tasks are not entirely compatible. That is to say, I believe that the most interesting artistic developments in China of the nineties exceed the conceptual framework of the panel. While this art exhibits many features which may be described as "modern," I do not think that they are, by and large, a direct result of the "reinvention of tradition," as the title of the panel might suggest. Here, then, I would like to offer some observations as to why this is so and, hopefully, to complicate the formulas by which we look at contemporary art in China and perhaps in Asia.

1
Fast Forward: The Contemporary Art Scene in Asia, symposium, organized by Asia Society, New York, and East Asian Studies Program, New York University, October 4-5, 1996. See "The Plurality of Contemporary Asian Art" for a discussion of the *Traditions/Tensions* exhibition. Eds.

Let me begin with a few words about non-official art in China. I use this term to refer to a type of art which first emerged in the late seventies and early eighties. Its appearance was made possible by decisive shifts in China's political climate. With the end of the Cultural Revolution and the tentative relaxation of state control, the possibility of an alternative cultural discourse emerged. For more than thirty years, the Communist state had sought to harness art in the service of the people and in the service of national politics. This policy and ideology was to be called into question by non-official art or avant-garde art, as it is commonly called in China. Seeking an artistic space of greater experimentation and greater autonomy from state dictates, non-official artists rejected the modes of Socialist Realism, academic art, and patriotic painting which had been enforced by the state for more than three decades.

Here, I have rehearsed a story which is probably familiar to many. What I would like to emphasize and to explore is the difficult relationship of this narrative to the paradigms of tradition and modernity. That there exists a category of art in China defined as non-official is in itself extremely telling. It alerts us to the unique social and institutional context that exists in post-Mao China—a context that is inextricable from China's socialist legacy. As the critic Xudong Zhang has stated: "It is through the socialist stage that China engages the external world in an unprecedented manner."[2] The first question that we must ask, then, is how socialism and its art forms—on the levels of practice, ideology, and policy—are to be understood in relation to modernity and tradition. It is from this vantage point that we can then come to terms with current developments in non-official art, which found its genesis as a reaction to dominant socialist forms.

2
Xudong Zhang, "On Some Motifs in the Chinese 'Cultural Fever' of the Late 1980s: Social Change, Ideology, and Theory," *Social Text* 39 (summer 1994), p. 131.

The answer that I would like to suggest to these questions is a schematic one, as more research and critical analysis needs to be done on the Maoist era and its repercussions in the cultural arena. For now, I would propose that the socialist legacy in China has been a highly ambiguous one. It may be argued that the Maoist revolutionary era belonged strictly neither to tradition nor to modernity. At the same time, it called upon and played out the logic of both of these categories. If tradition is to be understood as the ancient inheritance of a particular culture and modernity is to be understood broadly as the social and cultural forms associated with the imperative for future progress, then China's revolutionary era occupies an uncertain place in relation to both of these. At the same time that Maoist ideology mounted a sustained attack on the Chinese tradition—embodied in such "feudal" things as Confucianism, Buddhism, and literati forms of aesthetic contemplation—it also found in aspects of this tradition a source of continuity and legitimization. At the same time that it proclaimed a rhetoric of future advancement in a complete rupture from the Chinese past, state socialism under Mao also clearly deviated from the path of modernization as seen in Western capitalist society.

This ambiguity is reflected, to a certain extent, in the arts policy established under Mao. The primary official style adopted by the Communist government was Socialist Realism based on a Soviet model. At different times, however, the government also promoted woodblock prints derived from Chinese folk art as well as forms of traditional Chinese ink painting aimed at celebrating the people and landscape of China as a subject of patriotic pride. The Chinese government would, by turns, endorse or condemn the practice of traditional painting as a consequence of shifts in the political and ideological climate. These different trajectories reveal the complex intersection of the old and the new, of continuity and rupture, in the culture of the revolutionary era.

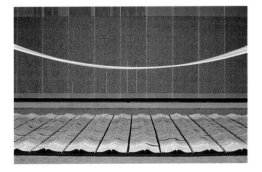

The ambiguity of China's socialist legacy sheds light on the cultural debate and artistic experimentation that would develop in the mid-eighties. By way of getting at these issues, let me turn to a specific work of art from that period— Xu Bing's *A Book from the Sky*.

Xu Bing
A Book from the Sky, 1987-1991 (detail)
Installation view, Elvehjem Museum of Art,
University of Wisconsin-Madison

109

First exhibited in China in 1988, this installation took the form of an all-enveloping textual environment. Massive sheets of Chinese characters were suspended from the ceiling, pasted on the wall, and laid on the floor. To produce the work, Xu Bing had spent three years hand-carving the individual printing blocks for four thousand characters. The surprising twist to this work is that the characters in *A Book from the Sky* are totally unintelligible. Though Xu Bing derived his lexicon from an authoritative Chinese dictionary, he subjected its parts to a radical *bricolage* in order to create a nonsense script.

Xu Bing's work has been the subject of a great deal of commentary in recent years. For many critics, it exemplifies the masterful blending of traditional Chinese thematics with a modern art form and is a testament to the continuity of the Chinese tradition in a modern guise. I would argue, however, that Xu Bing's work in fact contradicted such a reading. What interests me about this work is the way in which Xu Bing, so to speak, staged the reappearance of the Chinese tradition. While he constructed a symbolic text fully resonant of this tradition, he did so only to evacuate all meaning from such a text. In this paradoxical way, Xu Bing's work spoke to the predicament of the post-Mao generation in the mid-eighties. Here, modernism does not entail the reinvention of tradition as such, but rather the recognition of the impossibility of such a project. And that sense of impossibility is linked, as I've tried to suggest, to the socialist legacy which maintained the place of the Chinese tradition in its official culture only to radically reformulate or to deny many aspects of that inheritance. This legacy has made the search for an "authentic" or viable tradition in the post-Mao era a highly ambivalent and difficult task.

As we move from the eighties into the nineties, we witness a China which is undergoing an accelerated and often bewildering pace of change, with its rapid transition towards a market economy, its ongoing reconfiguration of central and regional power, and its broadening of contacts with the world outside. The picture has thus become even more complicated. The growth of a foreign as well as a domestic market for contemporary Chinese art, in particular, has had a significant impact on the institutional and social context of art-making in China. As a result, the position and meaning of non-official or avant-garde art has also changed. Given these complications and ongoing transformations, a thorough account of current developments in Chinese art would be impossible. Having made this caveat, let me suggest some ways of thinking about tradition and modernity in China in the nineties.

Looking at the art of the present decade in China, what strikes me is the absence of works which address the Chinese tradition with the degree of ambition and focus of Xu Bing's *A Book from the Sky*. (As an aside, let me add that my remarks pertain to avant-garde artists primarily based in China, rather than those—like Huang Yong Ping, Xu Bing, and Cai Guo Qiang—who subsequently emigrated in the late eighties and who address from this position a specific set of inter-cultural tensions.) This resistance or indifference to tradition by avant-garde artists in China has, I believe, partly to do with the contradictions of the socialist legacy as I have briefly outlined them. Moreover, as many critics have observed, China has witnessed a rising tide of nationalism in the nineties. In the place of Marxist ideology, nationalism has become the new banner cry. The potential alliance between nationalism and the reassertion of state power has made the invocation of tradition all the more suspect in the eyes of many avant-garde artists.

Chinese art of the nineties does exhibit, however, many features which may be described as "modern." If Chinese modernity in the nineties is not primarily a matter of reinventing tradition, then where is it to be

Wang Guanyi
The Great Criticism—Kodak, 1990
Oil on canvas
40 x 60"

located? The answer to this question returns us again to the socialist legacy that is still deeply etched in the landscape of post-Mao China. The most visible type of art which has come out of China in the nineties is Political Pop. This is a type of painting which reworks the popular imagery of the Socialist revolutionary era in an ironic commentary on the symbols of collective hope and unity—the heroic workers and national leaders that once emblazoned the billboards and public buildings in China. By juxtaposing these images with Western consumer logos, as in the work of Wang Guanyi, or by turning them into a decorative pastiche, as in the work of Yu Youhan, Political Pop undermines the idealized and iconic status of these revolutionary emblems. It may be said, then, that Political Pop addresses itself to the symbols and language of public discourse in China. By calling this discourse into doubt, Political Pop reveals the fundamental restructuring in the public sphere in China, with the waning of Marxist ideology.

What particularly interests me, however, is another type of art prevalent in China in the nineties which concerns itself, so to speak, with the other side of the equation, that is, with the sphere of the private. It is in this gap or struggle between the public and the private, I would like to suggest, that the modernity of Chinese art in the nineties can be found. Under the category of the private, I would include the many artists who explore questions of sexuality, memory, and other psychic

Cai Jin
Banana 58, 1995
Oil on Mattress
75 x 60"

Zhang Huan
12 square meters, May 13, 1994
Performance, Beijing, China

and physical coordinates of the self. Let me offer some examples. In her paintings done on old mattresses, for instance, Cai Jin conveys the complex dynamics of a woman's desire, which are unleashed through visceral images and garish colors but at the same time veiled in abstract form. In a performance done in a public toilet in 1994, the artist Zhang Huan coated his body with honey and fish oil and sat there for hours until his body was covered with hundreds of flies. As in his other performances, this project tested the ultimate limits of the body. In a series of paintings from 1994, Fang Lijun uses the image of a lone swimmer in a pool of brilliant blue

Song Dong
Breathing Out, 1996
Performance, Beijing, China

Fang Lijun
1994 No. 6, 1994
Oil on canvas
72 x 100"

113

Yin Xiuzhen
Wool, 1995
Wool, knitting needles
Dimensions variable

water to evoke a sense of isolation and estrangement. In a more conceptual vein, in the performances of Song Dong, we see the artist inscribing his presence with water or with his own breath on the ground, thus tracing the ephemeral coordinates of self-identity. In a piece by Yin Xiuzhen, the artist unravels old sweaters that had been stored in the family clothes chest to evoke the condensation of memory and the fragility of personal bonds. In another work, she documents all the gates and doorways in her everyday environment to map out a personal itinerary of liminal passage. In the work of Zhu Fadong, the quest for individual identity becomes an absurdist exercise. In one performance, he walked through the streets of Beijing on his back with a sign that read "This person for sale. Price to be discussed." In another, he published a missing person's ad for himself.

Zhu Fadong
This person is for sale, price negotiable, 1994
Performance, Beijing, China

Zhu Fadong
Announcement of Missing Person, 1993
Kunming, China

These works vary widely in terms of style and media. They are linked, however, by their focus on the individual and the intensely personal, which lies on the other side of Political Pop and thus links up in a different way with China's socialist legacy. What this type of art raises as a key issue in post-Mao China is the question of subjectivity. For at the heart of Maoist ideology was the ideal of collectivization which was to be extended to every sphere of life. In the revolutionary era, bourgeois subjectivism and idealism were thus consigned to the enemy camp. As the critic Liu Kang has observed, with the end of the Cultural Revolution, many intellectuals would launch a critique of Mao's legacy precisely on these terms.[3] Thus, the concept of subjectivity has become increasingly central in recent debates in a variety of fields including literature, history, and philosophy. In the eighties, for example, theorists in China

3
Liu Kang, "Subjectivity, Marxism, and Cultural Theory in China," in *Politics, Ideology and Literary Discourse in Modern China*, eds. Liu Kang and Xiao Bing Tang (Durham: Duke University Press, 1993).

Zhang Xiaogang
Bloodline: The Big Family, No.1, 1995
Oil on canvas
71 x 90 1/2"

Zhang Peili
Document on Hygiene No. 3, 1991
Video, 60 minutes

Geng Jianyi
The Reasonable Relationship, 1994
Performance, Hangzhou-Shanghai, China

inaugurated a heated discussion of humanism and individual consciousness within a Marxian framework. It is within the context of these developments revolving around the individual subject that I would place many Chinese artists working in the nineties.

In addition to those I have already mentioned, there are a number of artists who address quite specifically the role of subjectivity in the context of a socialist state. The poignancy and melancholy of Zhang Xiaogang's works, for example, has much to do with the tension between the personal and the anonymous. His paintings are modeled on found photographs from the period of the Cultural Revolution, which had proscribed poses and fixed formats. In this space of collective memory, Zhang also seeks to locate a place for private remembrance. From a different vantage point, Zhang Peili's videos reflect on the psychic after-effects of living under an authoritarian regime. In his work, Zhang constructs his narrative on the principle of repetition—the continuous movement of a wind-up toy and the repeated ritual of washing a chicken—to suggest the numbing boredom of daily routines and the paralysis of individual will. In a similar fashion, Geng Jianyi's work comments on the bureaucratic control of everyday life in a socialist state. In a performance piece from 1994, for example, Geng contracted someone to go to Shanghai for him because, as he writes, the artist suffers from intense paranoia. The surrogate was asked to keep detailed notes of everything she saw and ate.

By raising the question of subjectivity in post-Mao China, I do not want to suggest that Chinese art has suddenly adopted the myths of Western individualism or aesthetic self-expression in the nineties. Nor do I want to suggest that this work is overtly subversive or oppositional to the Communist regime. Rather, I want to point out some of the stress lines in the social geography of post-Mao China to which artists are currently responding. These stress lines may be traced to China's socialist legacy, which has combined with the country's rapid but uneven transformation towards a market economy to produce a social environment of contradiction and uncertainty. Working in post-Mao China, these artists reflect on the crisis of consciousness brought about by the realignment between self and society, the individual and the collective, the public and the private. As a result, artists have also turned to the space of everyday life in order to explore its shifting social, psychic, as well as physical dimensions. This is where I would locate the modernity of Chinese art in the nineties, in that the relationship between the private and the public, between art and the everyday, are also key issues for Western modern art, because of profound institutional and social changes that occurred beginning in the nineteenth century. The implication of these changes are still being revised and worked out by contemporary Western artists. It is for these reasons that I would argue that modernity in post-Mao China is not always the result of the "reinvention of tradition."

The parallels I have suggested do not mean, however, that modern Chinese art is reduplicating the path of modern Western art. Rather, I would agree with the critic Xudong Zhang who writes that "in this concrete context, modernity means an alternative modernity, originating in the socio-economic process of Chinese modernization that . . . [nonetheless] keeps a constructive dialogue with Euro-American modernism."[4] More broadly, I would like to suggest that the history of modernity has been largely written not only from the perspective of the West but also from the perspective of capitalist societies. With the end of the Cold War and the break-up of the former Soviet Union, not to mention the dramatic changes going on in China, we will need to rewrite that history.

1996

4
Zhang (summer 1994), p. 129.

High and Low: The Cultural Space
of Contemporary Taiwanese Art

In exploring the art of twentieth-century China, recent scholars have
challenged the notion of modernism as a strictly Western concept and
phenomenon by relocating modernism from the context of Euro-America
to that of China. I would like to further complicate this project by
addressing some constraints inherent in a Sino-centric framework. I am
interested in the possibility of a more local definition of the modern,
specifically in the contemporary art of Taiwan. As recent news events
have made clear, Taiwan occupies an uneasy political position in relation to China and has not been easily subsumed within China's national
narrative. In recent years, Taiwanese scholars and critics have begun to
formulate the terms of a Taiwanese cultural identity, an identity which
takes exception to the idea of a "Chinese essence."[1]

A group of Taiwanese artists whose work first gained prominence in
the 1980s and early-1990s illustrates these tensions. At first glance,
the work of these artists would seem to employ certain vocabularies
and motifs which belong to the "Chinese tradition." To interpret
their work in this way, however, would bring Taiwanese art back into
the fold of China's cultural embrace. It would once again privilege
China as orthodox center. By examining their art from a different
vantage point, I would like to challenge this paradigm and call into
question the continuity of the Chinese tradition in Taiwan. In so
doing, I hope to suggest some alternative ways of defining what is
modern about current Taiwanese art, without however resorting to a
strictly Western paradigm.

How, then, might one think about contemporary Taiwanese art beyond
the restrictive categories of the traditional versus the modern, or of the

1
Originally written as a paper
for the panel "Art and
Modernism in China, 1900-
97," College Art Association
conference, 1997. See *Credits*
for details. *Eds.*

Chinese versus the Western? For this particular group of contemporary Taiwanese artists, I would stress the importance of another kind of cultural axis. This axis extends, so to speak, from the high to the low and encompasses three cultural spheres—high culture, popular culture, and mass culture. Together, these three intersecting spheres map out the complex cultural and social space of contemporary Taiwan. And this space, I would like to suggest, has given rise to an art that is both distinctly Taiwanese and distinctly modern.

The work of Yu Peng, for example, draws readily from the vocabularies and techniques of Chinese ink painting but at the same time subtly undermines the authority of that tradition. And he does so, in part, by fusing the language of high art with that of popular art. Yu has keenly studied the mainstream tradition of Chinese literati ink painting, having lived around the corner from the National Palace Museum for most of his life. And he has referred to the landscapes of Ming and Qing masters as an inspiration and model for his own work. Yet, his work also contains many elements which exceed the norms of that tradition. In his paintings, the scale of figure to landscape is often deliberately exaggerated to the point of distortion. Pictorial elements are dispersed across the surface of his painting to create an extreme degree of spatial fragmentation. Or sometimes they are compressed so as to create an almost claustrophobic feeling of spatial congestion. His handling of the brush seems to verge on the clumsy sometimes, and the transition between ink tones and color values can often seem abrupt.

Yu Peng
Where Goes the Little Fairy, 1990 (detail)
Ink on paper
55 1/6 x 13 3/8" each
Courtesy Hanart Gallery, Taipei

Yu Peng has described his work through the traditional literati idea of *zhuo*, or "intentional awkwardness." At the same time, this quality of awkwardness has a great deal in common with the attributes of folk art. The influence of folk art on Yu's work can be discerned most clearly in the pair of paintings entitled *Where Goes the Little Fairy?*, 1990. The frontality and schematic composition of the figures, the bold contrast of brilliant colors, and the even pacing of pictorial motifs from top to bottom recall the conventions of folk art found in New Year prints and the decorative titles that adorn old temples and domestic dwellings in Taiwan.

Yu Peng has discussed his great attraction to folk art, particularly those forms associated with the rituals of weddings and funerals. Such folk rituals in Taiwan, I would add, often have an innately theatrical quality, complete with elaborate costumes and props. It is interesting, in this respect, to note that Yu also spent many years studying, performing, and teaching shadow puppet plays. Perhaps it is this interest in puppetry and rituals which accounts for what might be described as the theatricality of Yu's own paintings. In his work, one often finds figures and still-life elements arranged together in the shallow space of a stage-like setting. The small plants, folded screens, and other pieces of scaled-down furniture create a miniature world and an intimate backdrop for reverie, fantasy, and role-playing. In many of Yu's paintings, this interior world melds fluidly into the exterior world of mountains and trees. Blurring the boundaries between inside and outside, near and far, Yu heightens the illusory quality of his imaginary world.

Rendered as a form of theater or performance, Yu's work calls into question the stability of the Chinese ink painting tradition. In a sense, he transforms that tradition itself into a kind of fiction, by assembling its fragments together in ever-shifting combinations. In a similar fashion, the deliberately naïve quality of Yu's brushwork and composition works against the grain of mainstream Chinese ink painting, by subverting its standards of refinement and high polish. These elements, along with the tendency towards spatial fragmentation, accentuate the contingency of Chinese ink brush conventions. In this way, Yu highlights the displacement of that tradition into the modern world of Taiwan.

The dynamics at play in Yu's work may also be described in another way. In Taiwan, Chinese ink brush painting has come, in many respects, to represent the apogee of high art. With the establishment of the National Palace Museum in Taiwan, the nationalist government actively promoted Chinese ink painting in the postwar years as an important national patrimony. The status of Chinese ink painting was further secured by the large number of painters who fled from mainland China to Taiwan in the late forties. These painters, who tended to paint in a conservative manner, dominated the more powerful segment of the art world through their presence as jurors for official exhibitions and as high-level administrators in art institutions. Nurtured within the environment of postwar Taiwan, Yu's work shows great awareness of and even pays homage to the established canon of Chinese ink painting. But he has also found avenues for individual invention, beyond the constraints of academic rules, through the mediation of popular forms of folk art.

Huang Chih-yang
Work from the *Zoon* series, 1996
Ink on paper
Series of eleven works
133 x 50" each

Like Yu Peng, Huang Chih-yang also draws upon folk practices to create a distinctly personal style in the Chinese ink brush medium. Their works are stylistically quite distinct, however. While Yu's work is informed by a wide variety of folk art references, from New Year prints to shadow puppet plays, Huang quotes the symbolic idiom of religious talismans.

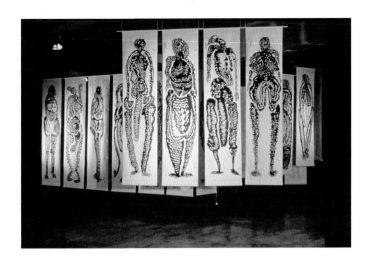

Huang Chih-yang
Maternity Room, 1992
Ink on paper
Series of twenty-seven works
23 5/8 x 94 1/2" each

In so doing, Huang has invented a new and transgressive vocabulary which exceeds the academic properties of Chinese ink painting he once studied in art school. In the monumental suite of paintings entitled *Maternity Room*, 1992, Huang employs an explosive brushwork to create a work of highly charged sexual inflections. The looming figures, half-animal and half-human, take form through energetic swirls of dense ink which recall the brushwork of Taoist talismans. As a medium which links the human world to the spirit world, Taoist talismans are intended to embody a powerful, material force. It is this somatic investment in the use of the brush which animates Huang's work as well, making his explicit sexual imagery even more visceral. Just as talismans ward off evil spirits, Huang's *Maternity Room* seems to function as a kind of exorcism. Huang views his work as a critique of the repressive nature of traditional mores and a commentary on the sexual and bodily anxieties of a changing modern society. And, in part, it is the example of folk practices which facilitates and enables this critique.

In highlighting the use of folk art in the work of Yu Peng and Huang Chih-yang, I would like to suggest that this is a distinctly Taiwanese phenomenon. Though historically related to mainland Chinese practices, the popular culture of folk art has evolved in quite specific ways in Taiwan. On an ethnographic level, first of all, scholars have discussed the unique visual and iconographic characteristics of Taiwanese folk art that have developed since these forms were first transplanted to Taiwan from China in the late Ming and early Qing dynasties. To focus on the indigenous characteristics of Taiwanese folk art in this way, though, is to fall back on a kind of ethnographic essentialism. Instead, I think we need to look at Taiwanese folk art from a social and historical perspective as well in order to understand its specificity to Taiwan.

One important dimension is the relationship of folk art to popular religion in Taiwan. In Taiwan, popular religion provides the forum for a rich array of folk aesthetic expressions, from ornate temple architecture and Taoist talismans to the colorful paper sculptures and costumes used in various funerary and Taoist rituals. The popular religion of Taiwan is closely related to that of southern Fujian. However, in Fujian as well as other parts of China, popular religion was largely suppressed by the Communist government until the 1980s. Only recently have these practices been slowly revitalized. By contrast, popular religion has flourished in Taiwan in the postwar years. As one scholar has observed: "In effect, two patterns of religious development have evolved, one in China itself, the 'Mainland,' and one in Taiwan, Hong Kong, and Singapore."[2]

2
Jordan Paper, "Religion," in *Handbook of Chinese Popular Culture*, eds. Wu Dingbo and Patrick Murphy (Westport, Conn.: Greenwood Press, 1994), p. 83.

The recent interest in Taiwanese folk art also has an important historical and ideological dimension. The study and revival of folk art in Taiwan can be traced to the 1970s. The diplomatic isolation occasioned by Taiwan's withdrawal from the United Nations in 1971, among other factors, prompted a period of self-awareness and reflection. As part of this "Nativist" movement in the 1970s, many scholars and critics began to explore the folk art of Taiwan as the basis of a local cultural consciousness. Within this context, the folk artist Hung Tung was particularly embraced by critics. Drawing upon popular mythologies and everyday visual motifs, his work was celebrated as an authentic document of life in Taiwan. Hung served as an important reference for the artists who emerged in the 1980s, a period during which interest in folk art deepened, particularly after the 1987 lifting of martial law and the rise of local political consciousness.

That Hung Tung was an outsider artist, a farmer who was largely self-taught, made him a figure of particular significance. The artists who followed him in the 1980s and 1990s have turned to folk art as a strategy for artistic critique and innovation, from outside the canons of both Chinese and Western art, so to speak. That this phenomenon is distinct to Taiwan becomes clear when we look at parallel developments in mainland China. Folk art has, of course, also played an important role in the art of mainland China in the twentieth century. Beginning in the late thirties, the Communist Party strongly advocated the use of folk art as a vehicle for mass communication and dissemination. Woodblock prints, which were developed along the line of traditional New Year prints, served to transmit the official ideology of the state to the populace. The Taiwanese government, by contrast, did not actively support folk art until the 1980s. The relative independence of folk art from the state and from the academy has made it much more available and enticing as a resource for contemporary artistic experimentation in Taiwan.

Hung Tung
Untitled, n.d.
Ink on paper
41 1/2 x 13 1/2"
Courtesy Taipei Gallery, New York

125

Thus far, I have examined the formation of folk art and popular culture in Taiwan as a distinctly Taiwanese phenomenon. Just as importantly, popular culture in Taiwan has also acquired features which make it a distinctly modern phenomenon. In the booming capitalist society of postwar Taiwan, the type of popular culture which I have discussed is no longer the special province of rural village communities. It has found new channels of transmission through the mass media, developed new hybrid forms that cater to the taste of urban audiences, and even begun to incorporate the technologies and imagery of a modern industrial society. In short, Taiwan has a thriving mass culture, into which the popular culture of folk art has been partially absorbed. Thus, pop singers issue records of old folk songs with a disco beat and sing to thousands in large arenas. Television stations broadcast Taiwanese puppet shows and opera in the afternoon, intermingled with commercials for motorcycles and instant noodles. A curious instance of this modern transformation of folk rituals is the organ-toting flower cars (*dianzhi huache*) used in funeral processions. Once used to transport mourners to cemeteries, these vehicles now carry hired singers and even traveling strip shows.

The work of Hou Chun-ming reflects this fusion of popular folk forms with mass culture. After graduating from art school in 1987, Hou became an avid student of popular religion and folk rituals in Taiwan, traveling throughout the island to observe all the major temple processions and feast days. From that experience, Hou evolved a body of work, like *Collecting Spirits*, 1993, which appropriated the form and iconography of ancient myths for a new critical purpose. With its cast of sexually mutant characters, *Collecting Spirits* comments on the conflict of power in contemporary Taiwan, on both sexual and political fronts.

Hou Chun-ming
Work from *Collecting Spirits* series, 1993
Print
Series of thirty-seven works
61 1/2 x 43" each

What is of particular interest to me, in the context of this discussion, is the work's affinities with mass cultural forms. While the stark, graphic quality of Hou's work is derived from traditional woodcuts, its use of visual satire and exaggeration comes from contemporary cartoons. And while the work adopts the format of a traditional Chinese book, complete with all the requisite textual headings and annotations, the immense scale of the work shares an affinity with modern billboards. More specifically, Hou's work incorporates current lingo and puns which come straight out of Taiwan's new media. Finally, the explicit sexual imagery of Hou's work may be compared to the garishness and raucousness of Taiwanese mass culture itself. As Hou has observed, the work owes as much to ancient Chinese myths as it does to the flower cars which carry strip tease shows through the streets of Taiwan

In a much more direct manner, Huang Chin-ho depicts this world of folk beliefs, translated into a modern industrial society. In works such as *Fire* of 1991,[3] Huang inserts Taoist symbols of prosperity and good fortune—peaches for longevity and sugarcane for luck—in a tawdry setting of strip clubs, fleshy bodies, and gaudy shop fronts. Huang has written of

3
Unfortunately, permission to reproduce this work was not granted at the time of the essay's original publication. *Eds.*

his search for a distinctly Taiwanese aesthetic. He states, "I seek to make an overall assessment of Taiwan's cultural tradition in order to open up new frontiers for the country's new aesthetics, which is distinct from those of China and the Western world." Judging by his paintings, it is precisely this combination of popular culture and Taoist folklore and the mass culture of heightened sexual and material consumption which has come to represent modern Taiwan for Huang Chin-ho.

By way of conclusion, I would like to return to the idea of "tradition." Fundamental to any narrative of nationhood, such as that of China, is the concept of tradition. It is against this tradition that definitions of the modern are often constructed. Such a view is problematic, however, for it posits a monolithic Chinese tradition, which is then rejected, harnessed, or modified for the sake of modernization. Working in the format of Chinese ink paintings and woodblocks, Yu Peng, Huang Chih-yang, and Hou Chun-ming all employ vocabularies and motifs which may be identified with that "tradition." However, there are alternative ways of understanding their art within a local Taiwanese context which question the dominance of the Chinese tradition.

1997

Modernism and the Chinese Other in Twentieth-Century Art Criticism[1]

1
Editors' title, the essay having been left provisionally untitled by the author. *Eds.*

On the other side of negation is always emptiness: that is a message which modernism never tires of repeating and a territory into which it regularly strays. We have an art in which ambiguity becomes infinite, which is on the verge of proposing—and does propose—an Other which is comfortably ineffable, a vacuity, a vagueness, a mere mysticism of sight.

T. J. Clark

Writing in 1982, T.J. Clark described the formalist tendencies of twentieth-century Western art and art criticism as an Other of modernism.[2] According to Clark, modernism is fundamentally a practice of negation, born of its estrangement from bourgeois society under the hegemony of modern capitalism. The turn to formalist concerns—to "the comfortably ineffable" and to "a mere mysticism of sight"—is at once a disavowal and a manifestation of this irrevocable predicament. And so it is the Other of modernism's true project of negation. Shattering the coherent guise that modernism once assumed, Clark evokes instead a historical practice rife with tension and contradiction.

2
T.J. Clark, "Clement Greenberg's Theory of Art," in *Pollock and After: The Critical Debate*, ed. Francis Frascina (New York: Harper and Row, 1985), pp. 59-60. First published in *Critical Inquiry* 9, no. 1 (September 1982), pp. 139-156.

Clark's turn of phrase is striking. It is also curious in view of recent critical theories which have addressed the problems of cultural difference through the figure of the Other. While Clark's interests lie elsewhere, his invocation of the Other in relation to formalism is, in fact, quite germane to such inquiries. For modernism's relationship with this Other—with the so-called Primitive art of Africa and Oceania and with the graphic art of Japan, for example—has often followed a similar trajectory whereby conflicting cultural values are neutralized under the accord of aesthetics. Such was the tactic, as Hal Foster and others have

129

argued, of the landmark 1984 exhibition, *"Primitivism" in 20th Century Art*, at the Museum of Modern Art. As Foster writes, it was the organizer's "absolution of (con)textual meanings and ideological problems in the self-sufficiency of form that allowed for the humanist presuppositions of the show (that the final criterion is Form, the only context Art, the primary subject Man.)"[3]

3
Hal Foster, "The 'Primitive' Unconscious of Modern Art, or White Skin Black Masks," in *Recodings: Art, Spectacle, Cultural Politics* (Seattle: Bay Press, 1985), p. 183.

This tendency is equally true of modernism's relationship with Chinese art. Though it has received comparatively less attention than its African or Japanese counterpart, Chinese art has also played a role, albeit intermittent, in the discourse of modern Western art. Over the years, it has been the subject of commentary by a number of critics who have been significant contributors to the critical development of Western art in the modern period. These include eminent critics like Roger Fry and Clement Greenberg, as well as more obscure figures like Georges Duthuit. More recently, the philosopher and critic Arthur Danto and the art historian Norman Bryson have also written about Chinese art in a continuation of or a response to their modernist legacy. While these writings vary in length and depth, ranging from short reviews to substantial monographs, they reveal a distinct pattern in the modern West's aesthetic fascination with China. As suggested already, this interest was most often couched in formalist terms, especially in the writings of someone like Roger Fry, for whom aesthetics was the means of negotiating the divide of cultural difference. Although later critics would deviate from and even challenge a strictly formalist reading of Chinese art, formalism has nonetheless left its mark. In this, a larger issue seems to have been at stake.

For the formalist enterprise entailed an important paradigm shift in Western modernism, by contesting the representational aims held to be the main historical legacy of Western art. That this function of visual representation—variously designated as mimesis, illusionism, realism, perceptualism, optical naturalism, or Cartesian perspectivalism—has come under repeated scrutiny and challenge reveals the West's continuing ambivalence about its aesthetic past. It is from this point of view, as we shall see, that Chinese art seems to have exerted its special appeal for critics of Western modern art. For them, Chinese art comes to signify, by turns, the promise as well as the hazards of surrendering this task of representation. It is in this way that Chinese art becomes the Other of Western modernism—an Other, to borrow T.J. Clark's words again, which becomes suspended in "a vacuity, a vagueness, a mere mysticism of sight."

In this foray into the *Other* history of modern Western art criticism, it is quite à propos to begin with Roger Fry. He has, of course, been long identified with the formalist origins of Western modernism. Fry's work on Chinese art, in its preoccupations and ambivalences, would also set an important precedent.[4] Though primarily known as a champion of Post-impressionism in England, Fry was versed in and wrote about a wide variety of art, from Italian quatrocento painting to Flemish drawings and African sculptures. He also developed an early interest in Chinese art and even acquired Han and Tang dynasty terra-cotta figures, among other objects, for his private art collection. Fry would find opportunity to write about Chinese art on a number of occasions throughout his career, whether by contributing exhibition reviews to magazines or prefaces to monographs and anthologies. His most sustained statement appeared in 1935, in the form of an introduction to a special issue of *Burlington Magazine* devoted to Chinese art.[5]

In this brief essay entitled "The Significance of Chinese Art," Fry presents a concise introduction aimed at those new to the art of China. In the form of a diagnostic primer, Fry's essay highlights three major formal

4
This is not to suggest that Fry was the first to have stressed the formalist approach to Chinese art. In Fry's time, this view of Asian art seems to have been prevalent, as suggested by early nineteenth-century art criticism cited in Jacqueline Falkenheim, *Roger Fry and the Beginnings of Formalist Art Criticism* (Ann Arbor, Mich.: UMI Research Press, 1980), pp. 11-12.

5
Roger Fry, "The Significance of Chinese Art." In 1946, B.T. Batsford reissued the 1935 volume under the title *Chinese Art: An Introductory Handbook to Painting, Sulpture, Ceramics, Textiles, Bronzes and Minor Arts*. All subsequent quotes from Fry's essay are from this edition.

attributes of Chinese art. The first is linear rhythm, which Fry describes as the main method of expression in Chinese art. As he writes: "The contour is always the most important feature of the form." Secondly, he notes that this rhythm has a continuous and flowing character. Thirdly, Fry identifies what he called "a peculiarity" in the plastic feeling of Chinese art. While Europeans conceive of three-dimensional form in terms of planes, Fry explains, the Chinese take as their point of departure "the sphere, the egg and the cylinder."[6]

6
Fry (1946), p. 2.

To a certain degree, Fry's observations are useful. They help to clarify, on a structural level, some of the organizational principles of the Chinese picture surface. Fry's interests are, nonetheless, restrictive. They are, after all, decidedly formalist. Throughout his essay, Fry offers a number of justifications for his approach, which point to a larger and more significant subtext. In essence, Fry's arguments revolve around the question of difference: How can Westerners appreciate the art of a culture so different from their own and why should they do so?

The trope of difference recurs throughout Fry's essay. As he states in the opening paragraph: "There are, I believe, many people well acquainted with some aspects of European art who still feel that the art of China is strange to them. For them to come upon a book like this is to come upon a world to which they have no key." With this rhetorical opening, Fry goes on to refute this perception of estrangement in the reminder of his essay. Chinese art can be accessible, he suggests, because formalism provides the means for bridging the gap of difference. It is on these grounds that Fry dismisses such issues as iconography and subject matter from his account. These aspects of Chinese art, in Fry's opinion, are simply too foreign for the Western viewer. He states: "A man need not be a Sinologist to understand the aesthetic appeal of a Chinese statue. It may represent some outlandish divinity, but it is expressed according to certain principles of design and by means of a definite rhythm."[7] Elaborating this point later in the essay, Fry observes: "In its formal aspects, then, Chinese art presents no serious difficulty to our European sensibility. I have admitted that much of its content is inspired by feelings which are not easily accessible to us, but it is really very difficult to us to enter into the psychology which lies behind much of our own medieval art."[8]

While Fry presented his aesthetic standards as universal, his evaluation of Chinese art was in fact largely determined by his pre-existing aesthetic interests in Western art. Many of the attributes that he identified in Chinese art were those which he had already highlighted in the study of Western art, both classical and modern. The concept of line and contour, for example, which Fry viewed as intrinsic to Chinese art, was a constant leitmotif in Fry's writings, developed in such early essays as "Line as a Means of Expression in Modern Art" of 1918.[9] Fry's interest in line, as one art historian has noted, was also a product of his early immersion in classical art and its long-standing debate over *disegno* versus *colore*.[10] Fusing together these disparate interests, Fry forged a totalizing theory which cut across different historical moments and different cultures. Thus he had observed in an essay of 1919 that it " is irrelevant to us to know whether . . . a . . . bowl was made seven hundred years ago in China, or in New York yesterday."[11]

Even so, Fry was not able to dismiss so completely or so easily the problem of difference in his essay. Fry returns to this question, again and again, at various points in his essay, almost obsessively. "Still, there is a difference," he writes on the first page. "We do recognize some peculiar flavor in almost any Chinese work of art." Later on in the text, he observes: "If I am right, we touch here on some profound difference in the creative methods and in the imaginative habits of European and

7
Fry (1946), p. 1.

8
Fry (1946), p. 4.

9
This was a two-part essay which appeared in *Burlington Magazine* 33 (1918), pp. 201-208 and 34 (1919), pp. 62-69.

10
Falkenheim (1980), p. 75.

11
Fry, "The Artist's Vision," in *Vision and Design* (London: Chatto and Windus, 1920). Quoted in Simon Watney, "The Connoisseur as Gourmet: The Aesthetics of Roger Fry and Clive Bell," in *Formations of Pleasure* (London: Routledge and Kegan Paul, 1983), p. 72.

12
Fry (1946), p. 4.

13
Falkenheim (1980), chs. 4 and 5.

14
Foster (1985), p. 198.

15
Background information about Duthuit is scant, especially in English language literature. In addition to his association with the Fauves, Duthuit was also a scholar and champion of Byzantine art. He is also remembered in France for his 1956 book, *Le musée inimaginable*, a three-volume attack on André Malraux's *Les voix du silence*. Unfortunately, the book is not available through American libraries. For a brief background on Duthuit and a bibliography of his writings, see Yves Bonnefoy's introduction to the collection of Duthuit's writings, *Représentation et présence: premiers écrits et travaux* (Paris: Flammarion, 1974). See also a profile of Duthuit in *Apollo* 78, no. 17 (July 1963), pp. 68-69.

16
George Heard Hamilton, review of *The Fauvist Painters*, *The Art Bulletin* 34, no. 4 (December 1952), p. 328.

Chinese artists."[12] (Though he does go on to minimize the extent of this aesthetic divide.) Despite the universalizing tendency of Fry's theory, he was nonetheless wedded to the notion of a distinct national essence, both in the arena of Chinese art and elsewhere. As one art historian has noted, Fry's analysis of French and British painting was also shaped and limited by his belief in the existence of national styles and characters.[13] Fry's theory was thus simultaneously universalist and essentialist. In this, Fry's essay reveals a paradox of the Western encounter with Chinese art, a paradox which Hal Foster has described, in relation to Primitivism, as "a fetishistic recognition-and-disavowal of difference."[14] Fry's ambivalences would be played out more explicitly by subsequent commentators. Caught always between the recognition and the disavowal of difference, each critic could only judge Chinese art in terms of an either/or—either as an analogue or as an antithesis of Western art, either as the triumph or as the failure of visual form relieved of its referent and, thus, of the task of representation understood as optical naturalism.

To trace this development, one might begin with the curious monograph, *Chinese Mysticism and Modern Painting*, published in 1936, a year after Fry's essay. Its author, Georges Duthuit, was something of an aesthete and polymath, known in his lifetime primarily for his essayistic pieces on Fauvism.[15] His professional association with the Fauves was further cemented by personal bonds when Duthuit became Matisse's son-in-law. Like Fry, then, Duthuit was intimately involved in Western modern art. His promotion of Fauvism brought him into close contact with many of the same artists championed by Fry. But Duthuit's book, while sharing Fry's interest in pure form, was a project of a different tenor. Where Fry's approach to Chinese art was systematic and concise, Duthuit's was diffuse and verbose. As George Heard Hamilton once observed, the French author was often "tripped up by the uncontrollable extravagances of his own well-stocked mind and imagination."[16]

These extravagances were no doubt encouraged by Duthuit's mystical bent, which guided his analysis of form. As the title of his book made clear, Duthuit viewed mysticism as an integral aspect of Chinese art. In China, Duthuit argued, art was "a means of communion with the universe as a whole. [The artist] seeks to control the mass of the forces which rule the earth, the heavens and his own consciousness." This was an art inspired, at its core, by "speculations so transcendental, mystical and metaphysical." More importantly, Duthuit saw this aesthetic communion as a liberation from pure mimesis. It offered an alternative way of establishing correspondences between the visual image and the exterior world. What is to be learned from Chinese art, Duthuit writes, is "that the artist withdraws from the world, that he stands aside from its changing scenes even after having much admired them, that he regards himself as an inventor."[17]

Portraying Chinese art as an alternative to mimesis in his book, Duthuit set out to establish its affinity with the types of modern Western art which he prized. He saw an essential resemblance, for example, between Seurat and Mi Fu (1052-1107/8): "Both relied on the expressive power of color to bring out the basic harmony of a series of related or con-trasted tone values."[18] The Chinese repertory of "expressionistic" lines, its concern with atmosphere rather than delineation, its complexity of spatial rhythms—these were all qualities that might be found in modern Western art. Duthuit drove home these parallels with copious illustra-tions juxtaposing various examples of Chinese art with their supposed Western counterparts—a [Buddhist] wall painting from Dunhuang with a Degas oil of dancers; a Muqi (thirteenth century) rendering of a monkey with a Bonnard portrait of a girl; a Song dynasty (960-1279) court painting of deer with a Vuillard landscape; a Mi Fu with a Seurat; a sixth-century Chinese painting of a dragon with a Masson painting of insects.[19]

17
Georges Duthuit, *Chinese Mysticism and Modern Painting* (Paris: Chroniques du Jour, 1936), p. 14.

18
Duthuit (1936), p. 79.

19
Duthuit's attribution and dat-ing of Chinese works of art contain, no doubt, many errors. They have not been thoroughly checked for the purpose of this essay.

135

Duthuit's book married well with his lifelong agenda to promote a non-mimetic art. As a champion of both Byzantine sculpture and Fauve painting, Duthuit advocated these arts, too, for their handling of form, mass, and color which were the conduits of an essential spirituality. Duthuit's anti-representational stance has been summarized in this way:

> One need only break with the desire to simulate a three-dimensional object on a flat surface, and "color values" will be able to exceed their mimetic demands "with a view to [creating] an entirely more rapid concordance, or harmony," that of the unity of everything—or rather of real-life experience, which consumes everything—in the flash of its coming-into-being. Representation is death. It diverts [us] from things toward meanings which alienate us from them.[20]

It is on account of such views that Duthuit earned the sobriquet "un ennemi de l'image" from the same art historian.[21]

While Fry suppressed content in his discussion of Chinese art, Duthuit cloaked it in hyperbole of the mystical. In so doing, both accentuated the non-representational qualities of Chinese art. His understanding of Chinese metaphysics nebulous at best, Duthuit ultimately reduced it within the scopic terms of Western art. In the final analysis, as Duthuit concludes, Chinese art takes "the risk of denying the truthfulness of appearances as they are recorded by the retina during our everyday existence." This is a tendency in Chinese aesthetics which artists like Matisse and Dérain would also adopt. "For them the expression is no longer furnished by the features of the model posing, but it springs from the assemblage of painted surfaces, equally flatly laid down, the empty spaces having the same importance as the full ones. . . . Here again there can be no question of measurements, or relationships, or scientific truth," Duthuit states emphatically.[22] Duthuit thus presented

20
"Que l'on rompe avec le désir de simuler un objet, tridimensionnel, sur une surface plane, et les 'valeurs colorées' pourront déborder leurs obligations mimétiques 'en vue d'un accord, d'une harmonie autrement rapide,' celle de l'unité de tout—ou plutôt du vécu, qui consume tout—dans l'éclair de sa formation. La représentation est la mort. Elle détourne des êtres au profit de significations qui nous en aliènent." Yves Bonnefoy, introduction to Duthuit (1974), p. 7. (Translation Editors).

21
This is the title of Yves Bonnefoy's introduction to Duthuit (1974).

22
Duthuit (1936), p. 90.

an image of Chinese art that internalized the modern West's rupture with optics and science as the basis of representational truth. For Duthuit, dialogue with the metaphysical was a replacement for observation of the physical. More than ever, pure form became the essential attribute of Chinese art.

In the forties, formalism would find perhaps its most eloquent and staunch advocate in the figure of Clement Greenberg. In line with Fry's stress on formal values, Greenberg developed a prescriptive ideology on behalf of abstract art. Like Fry and Duthuit before him, Greenberg initially harnessed Chinese art in the service of his narrative of Western modernism. References to Chinese art first appeared in Greenberg's landmark essay of 1940, "Toward a New Laocoon." Here, as the familiar argument goes, Greenberg presented the history of Western art as an evolution toward aesthetic purity. Before the avant-garde revolution, Western painting had subordinated painterly values to literary ones. It was an art of illusionism that had sunk into the anecdotal and the picturesque. What the avant-garde accomplished was a purification of the medium. As Greenberg proclaimed: "Purity in art consists in the acceptance, willing acceptance of the limitations of the medium of the specific art."[23]

In the context of this argument, Greenberg cites Chinese art to illustrate an alternative relationship between the literary and the visual: "In China, I believe, painting and sculpture became in the course of the development of culture the dominant arts," Greenberg writes. "There we see poetry given a role subordinate to them, and consequently assuming their limitations: the poem confines itself to the single moment of painting and to an emphasis on visual details."[24] While here Greenberg seems to acknowledge denotative meaning as a subordinate function of visual form in Chinese art, later in the essay he goes on to single out

23
Clement Greenberg: The Collected Essays and Criticism, vol. 1, ed. John O'Brian (Chicago and London: University of Chicago Press, 1986), p. 32.

24
Greenberg (1986), p. 25.

the latter as a source of independent value. "To prove that their concept of purity is something more than a bias in taste, painters point to Oriental, primitive and children's art as instances of the universality and naturalness and objectivity of their ideal of purity."[25] In Greenberg's scheme, Oriental art—i.e. Chinese art—thus confirmed the formal autonomy of the visual medium. Its formal attributes could, and had to be, judged on their own accord, severed from their signifying function.

By 1950, however, Greenberg's evaluation of Chinese art had taken a new turn. In a review of the influential book, *Principles of Chinese Painting* by George Rowley, Greenberg cast Chinese art in a much less positive light. Echoing Duthuit's views of a mystical East, Greenberg described Chinese art as one of "psychological refinement." This emphasis on the subjective could be conjoined with the "abstract quali- ties" of Chinese art to achieve masterful effects. "When it comes to the use of the brush," Greenberg states, "that use which conveys exact feel- ing with every touch and harmonizes each touch, as an individual facet of feeling, with the unifying emotion of the whole picture—then the Chinese masters certainly have no equals."[26] In passages such as this, Greenberg again highlighted the abstract and expressive, as opposed to the narrative or mimetic, qualities of Chinese art. Unlike Fry and Duthuit before him, however, Greenberg perceived a drastic difference between the Orient and the West. For they have, as he writes, "tried to subdue to consciousness quite different areas of experience. The West has devoted itself to history, the physical environment, and practical method; the Orientals have concentrated on religion, introspection, and aesthetic experience."[27] As Greenberg's distinctions between the Orient and the West implied, this was an art directed towards the inner rather than the outer, the subjective rather than the objective, introspection rather than description, amorphous feeling rather than physical fact.

25
Greenberg (1986), p. 32.

26
Clement Greenberg: The Collected Essays and Criticism, vol. 3, ed. John O'Brian (Chicago and London: University of Chicago Press, 1993), p. 44.

27
Greenberg (1993), p. 42.

On this basis, Greenberg directed some harsh judgments against Chinese art. Its problems hinged on one critical term—the "decorative." This was a condition which particularly plagued later Chinese art in its "decorative prettiness" and its "corruptedness."[28] As Greenberg saw it, this decorative quality was embedded within the heart of Chinese aesthetics itself. He writes:

> The absence of full color and strong modeling in Chinese painting and its, so to speak, passive naturalism gave the decorative a foothold from the beginning. The emphasis on brushstroke and subtlety of dark and light values, and the exploitation of empty space were equally important elements that of necessity resisted the decorative. In view of this, it is my hunch that Chinese painting became as decorative as it now seems only toward the end of its development two or three centuries ago.[29]

Despite its authoritative tone, Greenberg's pronouncement is beset by contradictions. Opposing the absence of modeling and the passive naturalism of Chinese art to its emphasis on brushstroke and its exploitation of empty space, Greenberg presents these as two antithetical facets of Chinese art. They are, in fact, two sides of the same coin. One could argue that it is the "passive" naturalism of Chinese art which allows for its elevation of empty space and brushstroke into "active" components of visual form.

The vehemence of Greenberg's views becomes more comprehensible when considered in light of his criticism of modern Western art, where the term "decorative" also surfaced regularly. In his writings, Greenberg had initially reserved the word as a term of approbation. As Donald Kuspit has written: "For Greenberg, the most autonomous, abstract, and modernist picture is the decorative picture."[30] This was particularly true

28
The decline of Chinese art is a theme that recurs quite often in the writings of Western critics. This seems to link up with larger issues of history and time in writings about Chinese art. For a brief overview of these issues, see Colin Mackerras, *Western Images of China* (Oxford: Oxford University Press, 1989).

29
Greenberg (1993), p. 43.

30
Donald Kuspit, *Clement Greenberg: Art Critic* (Madison: The University of Wisconsin Press, 1979), p. 59.

of the all-over painting. Where Western art was once devoted to dramatic depth, the uniform distribution of painterly marks in the all-over painting created a decorative surface, which became the new priority. Surface and decoration were, for Greenberg, synonymous. But there were also risks involved in a surface-oriented painting. It could become nothing more than "wallpaper patterns capable of being extended indefinitely."[31] Greenberg confronted this thorny problem in the essay "The Crisis of the Easel Picture" of 1948—two years before his review of Rowley's book on Chinese art—arguing for a type of Modernist art that would somehow reconcile the dramatic with the decorative.

31
Greenberg, "The Crisis of the Easel Picture," quoted in Kuspit (1979), p. 62.

Suffice it to say that the "decorative" remained a term of continuing difficulty and paradox through Greenberg's career. As he once stated: "Decoration is the specter that haunts modernist painting, and part of the latter's formal mission is to find ways of using the decorative against itself."[32] This too would seem to be Greenberg's view of Chinese art. Masterful in its orchestration of brushstrokes and tonal values, late Chinese art was nonetheless condemned to a "decorative prettiness." It is thus "the specter that haunts modernist painting"—the specter of an art which had allowed painterly purity to veer off-course. It was an object lesson in the perilous path of modernist art.

32
Greenberg, "Milton Avery," (*Arts Magazine* 32 [December 1957]), quoted in Kuspit, *Clement Greenberg*, p. 63.

In the years since Clement Greenberg wrote "The Crisis of the Easel Picture," formalism has undergone radical reappraisal. How has this affected writings about Chinese art by Western critics? While there have been ostensible changes in the critical approach to Chinese art, traces of Fry's and Greenberg's prohibitions also seem to linger. Such vestiges may be detected in the work of the philosopher and critic Arthur Danto, who has published three texts on Chinese art within the last decade. In "Ming and Qing Painting" of 1989, for example, Danto introduces the deconstructionist concept of intertextuality as a theoretical frame for his review of a Chinese art exhibition at the Metropolitan Museum of Art. "Intertextuality seems to me to fit Chinese painting to perfection," he declares.[33] Danto's adoption of this term helps to illuminate Chinese art as a highly coded practice. Yet, he goes on to draw a drastic conclusion. He writes:

> There really appears in traditional Chinese art very little by way of *hors-texte*. It is as though, entering the work of art, one entered an alternative world where substance was paper, silk, and ink, created alongside the real world, an aesthetic refuge from uncertainties and terrors, and disasters personal, political, or physical.[34]

Applying Derrida's notion of intertextuality in its strictest sense, Danto denies the possibility that art can be simultaneously inter- and extra-textual. That is to say, Danto fails to allow for a type of art that might comment on the "personal, political, or physical" *through* reference to pre-existing aesthetic conventions and models. In this text, the formalist interdiction against optical referentiality in Chinese art has only transformed itself into a fashionable lingo.

In his essay "Later Chinese Painting" of 1988, Danto presents a thesis more subtle in logic yet equally biased by the modernist debate. Here, Danto comments directly on the representational status of Chinese art. He argues that optical resemblance was not a priority in the aesthetic tradition of China, though its techniques were available. By the late nineteenth century, however, Chinese artists would come more and more to prize optical resemblance because of their exposure to Western imagery. "This flood of imagery," as Danto contends, was perhaps "appropriated just because the West had begun to be perceived as culturally superior in Chinese eyes."[35] Quoting the curator Wen Fong, Danto sums this period up as "terrible times" for China. Ironically, as

33
Arthur Danto, "Ming and Qing Paintings," in *Embodied Meanings: Critical Essays and Aesthetic Meditations* (New York: Farrar Straus Giroux, 1994), p. 32. This review of the exhibition, *Masterworks of Ming and Qing Painting from the Forbidden City*, at the Metropolitan Museum of Art was first published in *The Nation* in 1989.

34
Danto (1994), p. 33.

35
Danto, "Later Chinese Painting," in *Encounters and Reflections: Art in the Historical Present* (New York: Farrar Straus Giroux, 1990), p. 181. Danto discusses some of the same points in his essay "The Shape of Artistic Pasts, East and West," in *Culture and Modernity*, ed. E. Deutsch (Honolulu: University of Hawaii Press, 1991).

Danto writes, the West also experienced a drastic reversal in the priorities of its pictorial representation around the same time. Through the impact of Primitive and Japanese art, "a whole order of representation opened up for artists who learned from the fact that the Renaissance ideal had somehow become eroded." What resulted was "the unseating of optical criteria."[36] In the space of these few pages, Danto uses the occasion of an exhibition review to offer a sweeping assessment of the shape and meaning of modern history. In so doing, he grafts the development of both later Chinese and Western art onto a grand narrative of historical impasse and trauma.

For Danto, moreover, there is a lesson to be drawn from Chinese art in relation to the current condition of Western art. "This wonderful exhibition will enable us all to see ourselves a bit from the outside," Danto writes. "Its art world is curiously similar to our own."[37] For China was, in Danto's words, "an inadvertent laboratory of historically induced artistic experiments."[38] In the same manner, history has also forced Western art into a corner and demands its drastic reinvention. This quandary, as Danto has argued for more than two decades since his 1974 essay "The Transfiguration of the Commonplace," has been brought about by "the end of art" as the West has known it. Attributing his theory to the epi-phany of Andy Warhol's *Brillo Boxes*, Danto sees in this emblematic object the final transformation of art into pure philosophy, into the consciousness of its own process. For Warhol's *Brillo Boxes* was indiscernible from the "real thing" and was constituted as art solely through its own self-definition. Danto's theory, as one philosopher has noted, is "modernist in mentality."[39] Predicated on a linear progression of vanguard innovations and breakthroughs, Danto's theory maps out a modernist trajectory of ever-greater self-awareness in the utopian project of art.

36
Danto (1990), p. 180.

37
Danto (1990), p. 185.

38
Danto (1990), p. 182.

39
Daniel Herwitz, "The Beginning of the End: Danto on Postmodernism," in *Danto and His Critics*, ed. Mark Rollins (Oxford, U.K. and Cambridge, U.S.: Blackwell Publishers, 1993), p. 145.

In the context of the present survey of critics like Fry and Greenberg, it is striking that Danto hinges his theory on the problem of referentiality as understood in modernism. In his view, modern art reached its end when Warhol pushed the Western project of optical resemblance to the nth degree. As Danto has written: "What Warhol demonstrated was that anything, if a work of art, can be matched by something that looks just like it which is not one, so the difference between art and non-art cannot rest in what they have in common—and that will be everything that strikes the eye."[40] That difference can only lie in art's self-consciousness. The problem with Danto's theory is that it fails to acknowledge or allow for a different order of representation in the *Brillo Boxes*—that of simulation rather than *vraisemblance*. By pronouncing the end of optical realism, Danto ends up rehearsing the old modernist verdict of the death of representation.

In view of Danto's wider philosophical ruminations, the parallels he draws between the conditions of late Chinese art and current Western art bear further scrutiny. Danto's apocalyptic view of Western art history has, first of all, inflected his reading of late Chinese art history as a rupture brought about by the collision between the indigenous and the foreign, the internal and the external. To make sense of this break, moreover, Danto in effect places the art historical trajectories of late imperial China and the modern West in an inverse relationship. Where one had to confront optical realism, the other was to abandon it. In so doing, Danto can only read traditional Chinese aesthetics in terms of its *lack* in relation to optical realism. In this way, China becomes once again an Other to the West.

Like Danto, Norman Bryson also cites Chinese art as a counter-example to Western art's involvement with optical realism. However, he argues this point on grounds quite different from Danto's. The citation appears

40
"Narratives of the End of Art," in Danto (1990), p. 344.

briefly in Bryson's 1983 book, *Vision and Painting: The Logic of the Gaze*, as part of a semiotic critique of what he calls the "Perceptualist" account of Western art. To summarize a long and complex argument, Bryson's book attacks the conventional art historical reading of painting "as the record of a perception." In its place, Bryson offers a series of analyses of "the social character of the image and its reality as sign."[41] In the chapter "The Gaze and the Glance," more specifically, Bryson explores the status of the sign in Western representational painting by way of a short comparison with Chinese painting.

Western painting, Bryson writes, is predicated on "the disavowal of deictic reference, on the disappearance of the body as site of the image." That is to say that the painterly marks on the surface of Western painting serve to erase references to the spatial and temporal coordinates of its own making. In the Western tradition, the oil-paint medium is used to cover the surface below it and thus to conceal the labor of painting itself. This, Bryson declares, is a painting of the Gaze. Here, vision becomes transcendent through its disengagement from painting-as-process. In contrast, Chinese painting "has always selected forms that permit a maximum of integrity and visibility to the constitutive strokes of the brush."[42] The fluid traces of ink displays always "the body of labor" and "the work of production" unfolding in time and space. In this sense, it is a painting of the Glance. Because one must read the traces on a Chinese painting rhythmically and serially, "within the *durée* of process," the act of viewing becomes a somatic experience. Thus, painting of the Glance reintroduces the body of labor into vision.

With the aid of semiotics, Bryson offers a fresh approach to the discussion of representation. By calling optical realism into question as the only gauge for the signifying status of the sign, Bryson grants the possibility of an alternative order of representation in Chinese painting and

41
Norman Bryson, *Vision and Painting: The Logic of the Gaze* (New Haven and London: Yale University Press, 1983), p. xii.

42
Bryson (1983), p. 89.

breaks new critical ground relative to the likes of Greenberg or even
Danto. Does he then right the wrongs of modernism? Bryson's model is
problematic on several counts. By juxtaposing Western oil painting
with Chinese brush painting through his categories of the Gaze and the
Glance, Bryson reintroduces a binary opposition between the two
traditions. Bryson, as several critics have noted, conveniently ignores
features of Western and Chinese painting that do not fit neatly within
his paradigm. On the one hand, he disregards instances of Western
art—artist's drawings, etchings, and Romantic painting, for example—
in which the process of the artist's labor has always been considered
integral.[43] On the other hand, Bryson also overly idealizes Chinese
painting and fails to recognize the importance of established conventions and symbolic meanings in the system of mark-making in Chinese
painting. Ignoring such features, Bryson reduces the brush mark to
pure trace, to the index of a somatic experience.[44] In this way, Bryson
sets up Chinese painting once again "as a liberating alternative to the
totality of Western European art."[45]

Because of the narrow scope of his interests, Bryson produces, ironically,
a rather one-dimensional account of Chinese art. While mindful of what
he calls "the body of labor" in Chinese painting, he never fully delineates
this body in tangible terms. In other words, Bryson does not connect the
phenomenological body, engaged in the process of painting and viewing, with larger considerations of the social body or the political body.
These may be questions outside of Bryson's expertise. But, as a result,
his analysis performs an "abstractive" function akin to that of the formal-
ists that preceded him, by taking Chinese painting outside of its social
and historical context. Focusing on the immediacy of the visual sign,
Bryson ends up with, as one writer has noted, "a rather restrictive formalist view of the theories of language and culture that [he] deploys."[46]

43
These criticisms are made in
two reviews of Bryson's book:
Alex Potts, "Difficult Meanings," *Burlington Magazine*
129, no. 1006 (January
1987), p. 32; and David Ebitz,
The Art Bulletin 69, no. 1
(March 1987), p. 157.

44
David Clarke, "The Gaze and
the Glance: Competing
Understandings of Visuality in
the Theory and Practice of Late
Modernist Art," *Art History* 151
(March 1992), p. 94.

45
Potts (1987), p. 32.

46
Potts, (1987), p. 29. In this
respect, it is curious how
much Bryson can sometimes
sound like Fry. In his 1935
essay "The Significance of
Chinese Art," Fry too noted
the physical aspect of the
brush mark in Chinese art in
terms that presage Bryson,
writing: "A painting was
always conceived as the visible record of a rhythmic ges-
ture. It was the graph of a
dance executed by hand,"
(p.3).

In his attempt to present a totalizing theory, what Bryson ultimately fails to do is to take into account the full complexity of visual signs in Chinese art. That these signs can function on multiple registers—the referential and the abstract, the somatic and the optical, the analogical and the symbolic, the denotative and the connotative—has been ignored not only by Bryson but also by the critics before him in favor of a reductive view of Chinese art. In this way, the discourse of Western modernism has continually framed Chinese art in relation to its own crisis of representation. This tendency has, in turn, engendered another problem—the problem of representing Chinese art itself in Western criticism. How do we reframe this representation in ways that do not position Chinese art merely as the antithesis or as the analogue of Western art? That is the next difficult step.

1996

photo: David Lee

Alice Huei-Zu Yang was born on June 24, 1961 in Taipei, Taiwan. She moved to the U.S. in 1976 and graduated cum laude from Yale University in 1984 with a B.A. in art history. She joined the curatorial staff of The New Museum of Contemporary Art, New York, in 1988, becoming Assistant Curator in 1991. Her curatorial projects at The New Museum include the exhibitions: *Embodying Faith* (1991), *Skin Deep* (1993), and *The Final Frontier* (1993). In 1993, she entered the graduate program in art history at the Institute of Fine Arts, New York University, specializing in modern and contemporary art. She also continued to work actively as an independent critic and curator. At the time of her death on February 7, 1997, she had just completed her Ph.D. coursework and examination requirements, and had been newly appointed the Robert Lehman Curator and Curator of Collections and Exhibitions at the Parrish Art Museum, Southampton. The exhibition, *Tracing Taiwan: Contemporary Works on Paper*, which Alice Yang was in the process of organizing, opened as scheduled at The Drawing Center, New York, in June 1997.

Bibliography

Curatorial Publications

Su-Chen Hung: Sweet Red-2. Exhibition brochure. New York: The New Museum of Contemporary Art, 1987.

*Marie Bourget: When a Successful Monochrome is a Blind Work of Art...*Exhibition brochure. New York: Farideh-Cadot Gallery, 1987.

"Introduction." In *L'Observatoire*. Exhibition catalogue. New York: Farideh-Cadot Gallery, 1988.

The Window on Broadway: An Installation by General Idea. Exhibition brochure. New York: The New Museum of Contemporary Art, 1988.

Until That Last Breath: Women with AIDS and *Overlooked/Underplayed: Videos on Women and AIDS*. Exhibition brochure. New York: The New Museum of Contemporary Art, 1989.

Eat Me/Drink Me/Love Me: An Installation by Martha Fleming and Lyne Lapointe. Exhibition brochure. New York: The New Museum of Contemporary Art, 1989.

"America, America, This is You: The Camcorder and the Red, White and Blue." In *From Receiver to Remote*

Control: The TV Set. Exhibition catalogue. New York: The New Museum of Contemporary Art, 1989.

Artists' profiles (in Japanese). In *Beyond the Frame: The Transition from Modernism to Postmodernism in American Art*. Exhibition catalogue. Japan: Setagaya Art Museum, 1991.

Embodying Faith. Exhibition brochure. New York: The New Museum of Contemporary Art, 1991.

Pintura i Representació: An Installation by Perejaume. Exhibition brochure. New York: The New Museum of Contemporary Art, 1991.

"Portraits of the Dead: Postmortem Photography in Nineteenth-Century America." In *The Interrupted Life*. Exhibition catalogue. New York: The New Museum of Contemporary Art, 1991.

1+1+1: Works by Alfredo Jaar. Exhibition brochure. New York: The New Museum of Contemporary Art, 1992.

Skin Deep. Exhibition brochure. New York: The New Museum of Contemporary Art, 1993.

Oliver Herring. Exhibition brochure. New York: The New Museum of Contemporary Art, 1993.

The Final Frontier. Exhibition brochure. New York: The New Museum of Contemporary Art, 1993.

Andrea Zittel. Exhibition brochure. New York: The New Museum of Contemporary Art, 1993.

(with Jonathan Hay.) *Tracing Taiwan: Contemporary Works on Paper*. Exhibition catalogue. Including the essay "High and Low: The Cultural Space of Contemporary Taiwanese Art," and interviews with Hou Chun-ming, Hsu Yu-jen, and Yu Peng. New York: The Drawing Center, 1997. "High and Low" and "Interview with Hou Chun-ming" also in this volume.

Essays and Reviews

"On Kawara." Exhibition review. *Asian Art News* (Hong Kong) 3, no. 6 (November/December 1993). Also in this volume.

"Long Chin-san." Exhibition review. *Asian Art News* (Hong Kong) 3, no. 6 (November/December 1993). Also in this volume.

"Godzilla: The Anarchistic Lizard." *Asian Art News* (Hong Kong) 4, no. 1 (January/February 1994), supplement. Also in this volume.

"Siting China: On Migration and Displacement in Contemporary Art." *The New Museum Newsletter*. New York: The New Museum of Contemporary Art, 1994. Also in this volume.

"A Group Show: *We Are The Universe*." Exhibition review. *Asian Art News* (Hong Kong) 4, no. 2 (March/April 1994). Also in this volume.

"Looking for the Identity of Korean Art" (in Korean). Exhibition review. *Wolgan Misool: The Monthly Art Magazine* (Korea), April 1994. Also in this volume.

"Bing Lee." Exhibition review. *Asian Art News* (Hong Kong) 4, no. 3 (May/June 1994). Also in this volume.

"Kunie Sugiura." Exhibition review. *Asian Art News* (Hong Kong) 4, no. 3 (May/June 1994).

"Why Asia? " (in Chinese). *Hsiung Shih Art Monthly* (Taiwan) 283 (September 1994). Also in this volume.

"José Antonio Hernández-Diez." Exhibition review. *Art Nexus* (Columbia), no. 17 (July-September 1995).

"Disorienting Territories." Exhibition review. *ART AsiaPacific* (Australia) 3, no. 1 (1996). Also in this volume.

"Letting Go: The Work of Rirkrit Tiravanija." *ART AsiaPacific* (Australia) 3, no. 2 (1996). Also in this volume.

"Ping Chong." Exhibition review, under the title, "Chinoiserie." *ART AsiaPacific* (Australia) 3, no. 2 (1996). Also in this volume.

"Sowon Kwon's Interior Schemes." Exhibition review. *ART AsiaPacific* (Australia) 3, no. 4 (1996). Also in this volume.

"Chen Zhen." Exhibition review. *World Art* (Australia), no. 4 (1996). Also in this volume.

"The Plurality of Contemporary Asian Art." Exhibition review, under the title, "Brave New Faces: The 'Traditions/Tensions' Exhibition." *ART AsiaPacific* (Australia), no. 15 (1997). Also in this volume.

"Xu Bing: Rewriting Culture." In *In Between Limits*. Exhibition catalogue. Korea: Sonje Museum of Contemporary Art, 1997. Also in this volume.

"Asian American Exhibitions Reconsidered." In this volume.

"MSG: The Processed Art of Michael Joo." In this volume.

"Beyond Nation and Tradition: Art in Post-Mao China." In this volume.

"Modernism and the Chinese Other in Twentieth-Century Art Criticism." In this volume.

Selected Scholarly Papers (unpublished)

"Toward Zero: Monochrome Painting in Europe and America, 1955-1960," 1993.

"Femininity as Maternity: The Work of Mary Cassatt," 1994.

"In the Domain of Theater: Early Works by Jannis Kounellis, 1967-1975," 1995.

"Power and Powerlessness in the 1930s: Bataille, Masson, and *Acephale*," 1995.

"'Empty, Dumb, Hollow, and Mute': Shitao's *Album for Huang Lu* of 1694," 1995.

"Sophie Calle: Gazing the City," 1996.

Credits

"Letting Go: The Work of Rirkrit Tiravanija," originally published in *ART AsiaPacific* (Australia) 3, no. 2 (1996).

"MSG: The Processed Art of Michael Joo," unpublished, originally written for publication in *ART AsiaPacific*.

"Xu Bing: Rewriting Culture," originally published in *In Between Limits*, exhibition catalogue (Korea: Sonje Museum of Contemporary Art, 1997).

"Interview with Hou Chun-ming," originally published in *Tracing Taiwan: Contemporary Works on Paper*, exhibition catalogue (New York: The Drawing Center, 1997).

"On Kawara," originally published in *Asian Art News* (Hong Kong) 3, no. 6 (November/ December 1993).

"Long Chin-san," originally published in *Asian Art News* (Hong Kong) 3, no. 6 (November/ December 1993).

Bing Lee," originally published in *Asian Art News* (Hong Kong) 4, no. 3 (May/June 1994).

"Ping Chong," originally published in *ART AsiaPacific* (Australia) 3, no. 2 (1996), under the title, "Chinoiserie."

Sowon Kwon's Interior Schemes," originally published in *ART AsiaPacific* (Australia) 3, no. 4 (1996).

"Chen Zhen," originally published in *World Art* (Australia), no. 4 (1996).

"A Group Show: *We Are The Universe*," originally published in *Asian Art News* (Hong Kong) 4, no. 2 (March/April 1994).

"Looking for the Identity of Korean Art," originally published (in Korean) in *Wolgan Misool: The Monthly Art Magazine* (Korea), April 1994.

"Disorienting Territories," originally published in *ART AsiaPacific* (Australia) 3, no. 1 (1996).

"The Plurality of Contemporary Asian Art," originally published in *ART AsiaPacific* (Australia), no. 15 (1997), under the title, "Brave New Faces: The 'Traditions/Tensions' Exhibition."

"Godzilla: The Anarchistic Lizard," edited version originally published in *Asian Art News* (Hong Kong) 4, no. 1 (January/ February 1994), supplement.

"Asian American Exhibitions Reconsidered," originally presented as a paper for the panel "Imag(in)ing Ethnicity: Its Impact on Cultural Discourse and Production," *Beyond Boundaries: First National Asian American Arts Conference*, Asian Arts Alliance, New York, December 17-18, 1993.

"Siting China: On Migration and Displacement in Contemporary Art," originally presented as the session chair's introduction to the panel of the same name, College Art Association conference, New York, February 16-19, 1994; edited version published in *The New Museum Newsletter* (New York: The New Museum of Contemporary Art, 1994).

"Why Asia?," originally presented as a paper for a panel of the same name, Taipei Gallery, New York, April 15, 1994; subsequently published (in Chinese) in *Hsiung Shih Art Monthly* (Taiwan) 283 (September 1994).

"Beyond Nation and Tradition: Art in Post-Mao China," originally presented as a paper for the panel "Modernism and the Reinvention of 'Tradition,'" *Fast Forward: The Contemporary Art Scene in Asia*, symposium, Asia Society and East Asian Studies Program, New York University, October 4-5, 1996.

"High and Low: The Cultural Space of Contemporary Taiwanese Art," originally written as a paper for the panel "Art and Modernism in China, 1900-97," College Art Association conference, New York, February 15, 1997; subsequently published in *Tracing Taiwan: Contemporary Works on Paper*, exhibition catalogue (New York: The Drawing Center, 1997).